EASY STEPS TO

MANAGING
CYBER SECURITY
RISK

EDITED BY
JONATHAN REUVID

Legend Business Ltd, 107-111 Fleet Street, London, EC4A 2AB
info@legend-paperbooks.co.uk | www.legendpress.co.uk

Print ISBN 978-1-7871979-6-1
Ebook ISBN 978-1-7871979-5-4
Set in Times. Printing managed by Jellyfish Solutions Ltd
Cover design by Simon Levy | www.simonlevyassociates.co.uk

Publishers Note
Every possible effort has been made to ensure that the information
contained in this book is accurate at the time of going to press, and
the publishers and authors cannot accept responsibility for any errors
or omissions, however caused. No responsibility for loss or damage
occasioned to any person acting, or refraining from action, as a result of
the material in this publication can be accepted by the editor, the publisher
or any of the authors.

CONTENTS

FOREWORD

Not so long ago, looking after national security was an exclusive government responsibility. The digital age has changed that – and permanently. These days it is not just the organs of the state and its infrastructure which are the direct object of cyberattack, it is also the private sector, and at all levels. Individuals and corporate entities have of course always been expected to take reasonable precautions against crime but in the past they have not been called upon to be active players in helping create the framework for secure conditions. But as the private sector is both victim and solutions provider, partnership with government in combatting cyber predators on the economy and security of the nation has become essential. Indeed, it is not too much to say that good cyber security and cyber resilience have become a duty for the corporate sector to which these essays are addressed.

But, as the authors point out, not everyone has got the message. As three of them put it: "there is a schism between the reality of cyber security risk and the number of businesses engaging sufficiently seriously with the threat". Better reporting of breaches may account for some of the estimated rise in the huge losses attributable to cyber crime but, however one reads the figures, there is only one conclusion to draw:

we are currently losing the battle. The types of actors, their motives and their modus operandi vary, but they all have the following features in common: stealth in breaking in, difficulty of detection and attribution and, in consequence, a high likelihood of success at low cost.

The hackers' heavy advantage is not going to change in the foreseeable future. Self-protection against it is an imperative and a good deal more can be done to reduce the risk criminal hacking represents. These essays contain revealing analysis and helpful guidance directed primarily at senior management and the boardroom who, as the custodians of company assets and shareholder interest, properly carry the responsibility for managing cyber risk among others. Standard and Poor's will in future include adequate management of cyber risk in their ratings. No doubt other ratings agencies will follow suit.

The need for greater cyber resilience emerges as one of the other main themes. As the techniques adopted by cyber criminals continuously evolve and as corporate reliance on electronic systems becomes ever greater, cyber security cannot be either a stable state or perfect. So knowing what to do when a breach occurs, who should do it and whom should be told in what order, will be important in limiting the damage and may, indeed, be crucial to company survival. The financial penalties for losing personal data in the directly applicable EU Regulation, which will come into force before the UK leaves, are swingeing. So it's a good idea to learn the easy rather than the hard way.

Rt Hon Baroness Pauline Neville-Jones
Former Minister of State for Security and Counterterrorism

PART ONE

Cyber security –
No Longer an Option

1.1

INTRODUCTION TO CYBER SECURITY RISK

Ben Johnson, Sam Millar and Helen Vickers
DLA Piper UK

Cyber crime is a broad term encompassing any crime committed by way of a computer or the internet. We acknowledge that cyber crime is an extremely complex subject; however, we aim to provide readers with an introduction to cyber security risk and to emerging best practice. Cyber crime is a constantly evolving threat. Recent analysis shows that cyber crime cost the UK more than £1.5 billion in 2015.[1] Reading about high profile cyber breaches in the news is becoming the norm. Recent examples of victims of high-profile attacks include Ashley Madison and TalkTalk. The effects of these breaches are clear – a loss of customer data or disruption to service coupled with reputational damage. Often the reputational effects are the most damaging: months after the attack on TalkTalk, its stock market value was still almost £1 billion less than on the day the attack was announced.[2]

---

1 http://www.thetimes.co.uk/article/british-and-us-police-unite-to-tackle-threat-of-cybercrime-l9qh95jxb

2 Raconteur (distributed in *The Times*), *Cyber Security*, 8 March 2016, p. 3

As a result, cyber security is becoming a priority for many businesses. Some small businesses are going so far as to stock up on digital currencies to pay the ransoms of hackers in potential future cyber attacks.[3] However, despite the disruption and huge cost a cyber attack can cause to a business, many businesses are not taking the issue seriously enough.

In a recent survey undertaken for the Government, 69% of businesses said that cyber security was a high priority for senior managers. However, only 51% of companies have taken recommended actions to identify cyber risk. Only 29% have formal written cyber security policies. Only 10% have a formal incident management plan. This lack of vigilance seems entirely out of step with the fact that 65% of businesses surveyed had detected a cyber security breach or attack in the last year.[4] There are myriad statistics in a vast number of surveys relating to cyber security. Without listing them all, the pattern that emerges is that firms, on the whole, are not taking cyber security seriously enough.[5]

There is a schism between the reality of cyber security risk and the number of businesses engaging sufficiently seriously with the threat.

TYPES OF THREAT

There are manifest types of cyber-threats of which businesses should be wary. Some businesses are more at risk than others from certain types of threat.

---

3   http://www.cityam.com/242702/businesses-are-stockpiling-bitcoin-to-pay-hacking-ransoms

4   HM Government and Ipsos MORI, *2016 Cyber Security Breaches Survey 2016*, May 2016, p.1

5   For further reading of statistics, please see Marsh and the *Cyber Security Breaches Survey 2016*.

• **FRAUD**

The vast majority of cyber incidents fall into the category of fraudulent attacks. These include identity theft, attempts at extortion, and other crimes which specifically target individuals or employees.[6] Fraudulent attacks often take the form of phishing emails containing ransomware which are sent to employees. A high-ranking employee or executive could receive an email saying that a significant amount of sensitive data has been stolen and will be released publicly on a certain date unless a large sum is paid. The deadline will rarely allow sufficient time for the investigation of such an incident.[7] Cyber-attackers in these cases are most often motivated by money.

THEFT OF PAYMENT CARD DATA

As we all know, criminals will frequently target locations where they can obtain the most money quickly. Cyber-criminals are no different and arguably, theft of payment card data was the forerunner to what we know as cyber crime today. Criminal gangs are able to launch cyber attacks on businesses which accept or process card payments; for example, by hacking into till systems and leaving software capable of sitting undetected in a system whilst copying card details before that data is extracted to the criminal. Such data is then sold through web-sites to others who are capable of creating plastic cards which are then used to make expensive purchases in countries where PIN numbers are not required.

Card data compromise remains one of the largest areas of potential liability for any party in the payment chain and accordingly careful steps must be taken to guard against

---

6   Marsh, *Cyber and the City*, May 2016, p5

7   Mandiant, *M-Trends 2016*, February 2016 p. 10

losses. We identify below some of the key issues arising in this area.

MERCHANT ACQUIRER OBLIGATIONS

Visa, MasterCard and other card schemes impose upon their merchant acquirer (payment processor) the obligation of ensuring payment card data security of merchants (entities accepting payment cards). The card schemes also administer, as part of their membership rules, methods of fining members who do not comply with data security obligations, and ensuring card issuers are compensated for losses arising from card data breaches.

Acquirers will then impose contractual obligations on merchants to ensure card data is kept securely and will require an indemnity for losses which result from a breach. It is important to understand the potential magnitude of such losses.

PCIDSS COMPLIANCE

Irrespective of whether a data compromise has occurred, the card schemes require members to ensure that they and merchants and third parties handling data on their behalf comply with the Payment Card Industry Data Security Standards ("PCIDSS"). This is a set of standardised obligations (often updated) regarding data security that a number of card schemes (Visa and MasterCard included) agree to enforce. Examples of obligations are: (i) installing appropriate firewalls; (ii) ensuring public access to systems is controlled; (iii) changing vendor passwords on software etc. This information can be accessed at www.pcidss.co.uk.

POTENTIAL LIABILITIES

As acquirers will pass liabilities arising from payment card data breaches to merchants, it is important to understand what these losses may be. These will equate to:

- Significant fines for failing to ensure a merchant is compliant with PCIDSS. It is worth noting that attaining PCIDSS compliance on any particular data does not provide a merchant with protection. Should a data compromise occur in respect of its card data, then there is real risk that a breach of PCIDSS is assumed.
- Card Schemes mandate immediate and urgent forensic investigation of events and the costs of that forensic investigation will be borne by the merchant. Obligations can include requiring a merchant to identify, contain and mitigate the incident, secure all card data and preserve all information/evidence concerning the event within 24 hours. It must document all actions and not reboot any systems. Card Schemes must be constantly updated. Remediation plans must be implemented in a matter of days.
- Card Schemes maintain a process which means they will manage the recovery of losses which Card Issuing banks have incurred as a result of the payment card data breach. These amount to fraud losses that cardholders suffer whilst criminals utilise their card numbers to make purchases.
- Other losses which card schemes enable recovery of are the additional costs which card issuers have suffered for:

  - Reissuing potentially compromised cards; and
  - Heightened monitoring of non-reissued cards.

Losses can run into millions of pounds and the consequences of an incident do not stop there. Given the significant impact card data loss might have on your business, it is imperative that steps are taken to comply with PCIDSS to ensure the security of systems and those with whom you contract to receive services. If in doubt engage with the rules and your payment processor, who will be able to guide you as needed.

TERMINATION

A retailer can easily find their merchant services agreement terminated due to breach of contract. The Card Schemes operate systems which can make obtaining another facility difficult when you have been terminated for breach of contract and accordingly, suffering a payment card data breach can spell the end of a business.

• DISRUPTION

Disruptive cyber attacks are intended to severely disrupt a business' operations. These can be instigated by certain agencies, governments, or even sophisticated terrorist groups, using the attacks as a way to make their presence felt.[8] For example, the North Korean government's disruptive cyber attack on Sony Pictures in relation to the film *The Dictator* intended to express its distaste for the depiction of Kim Jong-Un. Such attacks are also undertaken by political groups; for example, part of the Anonymous 'hacktivist' network took down the London Stock Exchange's website for more than two hours as part of its campaign against the world's banks

---

8   Raconteur (distributed in *The Times*), *Cyber Security*, 8 March 2016, p. 3

and financial institutions.[9] Disruptive attacks may also be undertaken for commercial gain.

• SYSTEM FAILURE

This type of cyber attack would cause an incident affecting multiple jurisdictions. This could take the form of a concerted attack on several firms, the failure of the payments system of a financial institution or the failure of Critical National Infrastructure. There are few cyber-attackers who have the motivation, resources and capability to carry out such an attack.[10] The consequences of such an attack would be vast.

• INSIDER THREAT

Firms must also consider the threat from within their organisations – the insider threat. An insider is defined as a person who exploits, or has the intention to exploit, their legitimate access to an organisation's assets for unauthorised purposes.[11] The insider threat comes from an employee or contractor – anyone with access to a site who could carry out cyber attacks. Insider incidents can be categorised into five main types:

- The unauthorised disclosure of sensitive information to a third party such as the media;
- Process corruption – illegitimately altering an internal process or system to achieve a specific, non-authorised objective;

---

9   http://www.cityam.com/242614/hackers-reportedly-took-down-the-london-stock-exchange-website-last-week

10   Marsh, *Cyber and the City*, May 2016, p5

11   CPNI, *Insider Data Collection Study*, April 2013, p. 4

- Facilitating third party access to an organisation's assets (assets including premises, information and people);
- Physical sabotage – tampering with equipment vital to the operation of the organisation;
- Electronic or IT sabotage.[1]

There are various motivations for insiders who commit cyber attacks. These may be malicious attacks, carried out by a disgruntled employee with the intention of extracting money from the firm or disrupting the business. There may be elements of corporate espionage or sabotage – a firm placing a contractor in an organisation in order to extract sensitive data. Vulnerable employees may also be exploited by someone who wishes to extract information from an organisation. However, insider threat can also be unintentional – the unwitting removal of sensitive data. It may be the case that this happens as a result of a poor recruitment process by which a particular candidate's suitability for the job has not been fully considered. 95% of all cyber incidents involve human error.[2]

• TRENDS

Cyber threats are credible threats for all businesses as well as individuals, whether it be a business held to ransom after the theft of sensitive information or a phishing email leading to a personal bank account being compromised. There are, however, certain sectors or industries which will be more vulnerable to particular types of cyber crime. The sector or industry also determines which type of information is the most valuable and, as a result, damaging if compromised by cyber attack.

---

1 CPNI, *Insider Data Collection Study*, April 2013, p. 4
2 Marsh, *Cyber and the City*, May 2016, p. 7

The financial services sector is an enticing target for cyber-criminals because financial services firms tend to hold large amounts of sensitive data.[3] A disruptive attack resulting in a firm's inability to store or transmit sensitive data would have a huge impact. For example, if a large bank's systems were compromised, this would affect businesses as well as individuals whose bank accounts would be rendered unusable.

Similarly, the healthcare, communications, media and technology and retail industries would be greatly affected by a disruption to their systems.[4] For technology and defence firms, the theft of intellectual property is a hidden cyber risk.[5] These are breaches which are unlikely to be reported because of the confidential nature of the industries involved.

A recent survey conducted for the Government sets out interesting trends in the types of attacks which firms in different industries are experiencing.[6] Administration or Real Estate firms were most likely to suffer viruses, spyware or malware. They were also more likely to have money stolen electronically. Information, communication or utility firms were most likely to have breaches relating to personally owned devices used in the workplace. Businesses in the financial or insurance sectors were most likely to suffer from impersonation in emails or online. It is clear that cyber-criminals are specifically targeting attacks to match with certain industries – an indicator of the ever-evolving threat that cyber attacks pose to businesses around the globe.

---

3   Marsh, *Cyber and the City*, May 2016, p. 9

4   Marsh, *Cyber and the City*, May 2016, p. 11

5   Marsh, *Cyber and the City*, May 2016, p. 12

6   HM Government and Ipsos MORI, *2016 Cyber Security Breaches Survey 2016*, May 2016, p. 35

UK RESPONSE

The UK National Computer Emergency Response Team (CERT-UK) was formed in 2014 in response to the National Cyber Security Strategy, which set out the importance of strengthening the UK's response to cyber incidents. CERT-UK's four main responsibilities are: (i) national cyber security incident management, (ii) support for Critical National Infrastructure companies in handling cyber security incidents, (iii) to promote cyber security situational awareness across industry, academia and the public sector, and (iv) to provide the single international point of contact for co-ordination and collaboration between national CERTs.[7]

The Council of Registered Ethical Security Testers (CREST) is the professional body representing the technical security industry. It assures the processes and procedures of member organisations, validates the competence of their technical security staff, and provides recognised professional qualifications and ongoing professional development for people working in the information security industry. Penetrating testing services are provided with guarantees that the work will be carried out by individuals with up-to-date knowledge of the latest vulnerabilities and techniques used by attackers.[8]

CREST and the UK Financial Authorities have launched the CBEST Vulnerability Testing Framework.[9] This is a testing framework utilising real threat intelligence which is

---

7   https://www.cert.gov.uk/what-we-do/preventing-cyber-issues/other-sources-of-advice/

8   https://www.cert.gov.uk/what-we-do/preventing-cyber-issues/other-sources-of-advice/

9   http://www.bankofengland.co.uk/financialstability/fsc/Pages/cbest.aspx

intended to improve the understanding of boards of financial firms of the cyber risks they may be susceptible to. It replicates techniques potential attackers use in order to test how easily they can penetrate a firm's defences.

The Cyber-security Information Sharing Partnership (CiSP) is a joint industry/government initiative to share cyber threat and vulnerability information so as to increase overall situational awareness of the cyber threat. The aim is that this will reduce the impact on UK businesses. CiSP allows members across sectors to exchange cyber- threat information whilst protecting the confidentiality of information shared.[10]

The Centre for the Protection of National Infrastructure (CPNI) focuses mainly on companies which directly provide Critical National Infrastructure. However, it has a variety of guidance documents aimed at instilling best practice and raising awareness of current issues related to information security.[11]

The Department for Business, Innovation and Skills (BIS) has published guidance to help businesses manage the cyber security threat. Its "10 Steps to Cyber Security" aims to help businesses prevent or deter most cyber attacks. The Executive Companion also offers guidance on how to make the UK's networks more resilient and protect key information assets against cyber threats. It covers risk management and corporate governance as well as including case studies based on real events. BIS have also issued a publication setting out guidelines for small businesses on cyber security.

As the threat from cyber attacks has grown, the mood in the UK has shifted towards identifying accountability for

---

10   https://www.cert.gov.uk/what-we-do/preventing-cyber-issues/other-sources-of-advice/

11   https://www.cert.gov.uk/what-we-do/preventing-cyber-issues/other-sources-of-advice/

breaches. The Culture, Media and Sport Select Committee recently recommended that CEO's pay should be directly linked to effective cyber security and that companies should be fined for delays in reporting breaches.[12]

The General Data Protection Regulation[13] imposes fines of up to 4% of global turnover for privacy non-compliance. For further information, please see chapter 4.

The Information Commissioner (ICO) is responsible for enforcing the UK's Data Protection Act 1998. Mandatory reporting is not currently in place for losses of data or other impacts of a cyber attack (except for telecoms companies). Guidance, however, suggests that breaches should be reported.[14] The ICO has a number of tools at its disposal to regulate organisations and businesses that collect, use and keep personal information, including criminal prosecution and the power to serve a monetary penalty notice on a data controller.[15]

British police have recently joined forces with their US counterparts to form the Global Cyber Alliance, made up of police specialists and industry professionals, who will identify the biggest fraud threats before putting together solutions for the business world.[16] This is indicative of an increasingly collaborative approach to fighting cyber crime, both between industry and government, as well as across borders.

---

12 http://news.sky.com/story/1714528/mps-mps-fine-firms-for-cyber-security-failures

13 Regulation (EU) 2016/679

14 Marsh, *Cyber and the City*, May 2016, p. 14

15 https://www.cert.gov.uk/what-we-do/preventing-cyber-issues/other-sources-of-advice/

16 http://www.thetimes.co.uk/article/british-and-us-police-unite-to-tackle-threat-of-cybercrime-l9qh95jxb

EU

The European Union's Cyber Security Strategy[17] has outlined the following priorities for its Member States:

- Achieving cyber resilience;
- Drastically reducing cyber crime;
- Developing cyber defence policy and capabilities related to the Common Security and Defence Policy (CSDP);
- Developing the industrial and technological resources for cyber security; and
- Establishing a coherent international cyber space policy for the European Union and promote core EU values.

This shapes much of its policy, as it drives to ensure that its core values apply in the digital world as they do in the physical world.

The European Commission launched a Directive on Network and Information Security in 2013.[18] For further information on this and the EU regulatory position in light of the Brexit negotiations, please see chapter 4.

USA

The Cyber security Act 2015[19] was the subject of much controversy before eventually being signed into law on 18 December 2015. Similar legislation was proposed in Congress with little success. Its aim is to encourage voluntary

---

17   https://eeas.europa.eu/policies/eu-cyber-security/cybsec_comm_en.pdf

18   Directive (EU) 2016/1148

19   Cyber security Information Sharing Act ‚s754, 114th Congress, 1st Session

information sharing as a means of defence against cyber attacks. Such information sharing would take place between government agencies, businesses and other organisations. The intention is that the sharing of information will allow businesses and other groups to identify hackers and defend themselves against cyber attacks. The measures introduced allow companies to share threat indicators and defensive measures with the US federal government, but they must also institute appropriate security controls and remove personal information which is not directly related to the reported cyber security threat.[20] The removal of personal information from data shared by businesses with the federal government may, to an extent, appease those who had expressed privacy concerns with regards to previous legislative proposals on the same topic. The Act also promotes and facilitates the sharing of cyber threat indicators and defensive measures within the federal government. This includes the sharing of classified information with relevant federal entities with the requisite security clearances.

There are a variety of organisations in the United States whose remit involves cyber regulation.[21]

The Department of Homeland Security, the FBI, the NSA and the Department of Defence view cyber primarily as a national security issue. As a result, they are keen for the private sector to provide them with as much information about hacking activity as possible. The Department of Homeland Security works with other federal agencies to conduct investigations and combat cyber crime. Some of its components, such as the US Secret Service and US

---

20   http://www.isaca.org/cyber/Documents/CSX-Special-Report_misc_Eng_0116.pdf, p. 3

21   This section draws heavily from Marsh, *Cyber and the City*, May 2016, p. 15

Immigration and Customs Enforcement, have special divisions which are dedicated to combating cyber crime. The FBI also has its own cyber crime division. The NSA has recently reached out to Silicon Valley based technology firms, imploring them to work together with the NSA to tackle cyber security threats more effectively.[1]

From a consumer protection stand point, the Federal Trade Commission and the attorney generals take the view that banks must tighten their digital security. This has an impact on the willingness of firms to disclose attacks.

With regards to financial services stability, the SEC and FINRA are happy to be punitive on firms with deficient systems, while working with them on disclosure and other issues.

CONCLUSION

As the cyber threat continues to evolve, so will the regulatory framework. One thing is clear – businesses must engage with the reality of cyber crime sooner rather than later.

---

1   http://www.networkworld.com/article/3040175/security/nsa-asks-silicon-valley-to-help-fight-cybercrime-terrorism.html

1.2

THE COST OF CYBER CRIME

Jerome Vincent, AXELOS Global Best Practice

(An interview with Jim Baines, CEO, Baines Packaging, Peekskill, New York)

Cyber crime has quantifiable costs – financial loss, IP theft or the compromise of confidential data. But the most devastating loss is often the most intangible: the reputation - of the brand and, most painfully, of an individual.

"I remember doing Shakespeare's *Othello* at school in England," says Jim Baines, CEO of the packaging company he founded two decades ago and built to become a respected market leader in its field. "Othello laments his loss of reputation. His status as a war hero and a great general is lost because he believes that his wife, Desdemona, is unfaithful to him. As a kid I couldn't connect with that sense of loss. I didn't understand why he was so worked up about it. Surely, the fact that he might have been betrayed by his wife was bad enough. What did it matter what other people thought of him?"

Jim smiles, and sits back in his creaking office chair stretching his arms out wide and taking a deep, almost baleful, breath.

"Of course, now I know. Now, I understand what was behind Shakespeare's writing. A kid doesn't quite understand a concept like 'reputation' because even if you have one – for being, say, a good ball player – you haven't spent years building it up. So, one bad game or two is easy to brush off. But, when people look at you and say – 'that's the guy who let the hackers into his own company' – then you really know how Othello felt."

Jim Baines' reputation is being repaired. Not just because he's getting his company back on track after a serious cyber security breach, but because he's willing to talk openly and honestly about what happened – and how it was his fault (mostly).

"Until it happened I didn't realise that I was a 'whale'. A big, juicy CEO target for hackers looking to exploit human weaknesses to get something valuable," says Jim. He has a wry smile on his face. "I wasn't even the biggest whale in the sea. The c-level executives in the large companies I supplied were the real targets. Multinational food companies, pharmaceutical companies, and retailers. But it was my carelessness that let them in."

A SALUTARY EXPERIENCE

Jim says he's learned a lot from his experience as a 'whale'. The hack began as a simple email purporting to be from an old friend which offered pictures taken at a corporate golf-trip in Hawaii. "It was a good old fashioned junket," remembers Jim, "and I'd played like Rory McIlroy – brilliant in an erratic kind of way." Jim laughs and waits to see if I get his reference to the sporadic genius of the greens. I do, just about.

"There was this one hole – a difficult one on a windy day – that I'd birdied. I posed triumphantly with the little flag in my hand. And later this email comes in with, I was promised, great pictures of that moment." The pictures were there – but only after Jim had clicked through an innocuous looking link. "I did what they always tell you not to do," he says, still obviously feeling a painful twinge of regret. He shakes his head. Then sighs.

"The rest, as they say, is history. My history. My painful history. I'd done it on my company laptop. The security policies that I'd signed off on in my own company were clear that I should never click on a link in an email without checking it first. But, I thought I was special. I was CEO. I could do what I wanted. I was exempt. Big mistake."

C-Level Executives Are Particularly Vulnerable

Since the hack – and the inevitable publicity that came with it – Jim has been vocal in his warnings to c-level executives. He talks about what he calls 'The Systemic Risk of Entitled Executives.' He likes to point out that the hackers target high-level managers and directors not just because they know where all the secrets are – many of their staff do too. But unlike other employees, high-level executives believe that they are entitled to a position of greater trust and are more 'relaxed' about observing security protocol, which means that they get careless more easily.

"It's a basic human trait. You know how you read about some high-flying politician or business leader who seems to be so slick and in control, but then gets careless. They walk out of a summit meeting holding papers so they can be seen. A photographer snaps them, and the contents of a confidential memo are all over the papers. A proposed merger or boardroom reshuffle is revealed. You know, it's really no different in the digital world." Jim taps his desk and seems to run through more examples, but resists the temptation to labour the point.

"You say to yourself, 'What was he thinking?!' And you can't believe that a guy like that – with so much savvy, could do something as basically naive," Jim says. "There comes a point when you take your position for granted, and you get complacent. Now, I didn't do something as obviously careless as that – but what I did actually almost cost me my livelihood and that of my workers."

Jim emphasises the reputational damage in many of his talks on the subject because he believes that the press coverage of cyber crime is too focused on the hackers and their criminal objectives.

"If you think about your reputation as well as the cost to the bottom line, then you're more likely to take the right measures to protect them both," says Jim. It's a line he uses a lot. He advocates adding his 'Systemic Risk of Entitled Executives' to the text book accounts of cyber security. "I know it probably doesn't sound quite right, but it's a more useful concept than much of the dry, tech-jargon you often get in articles about how to keep your company safe."

SECURITY PROFESSIONALS COMPOUND THE PROBLEMS

Jim faults the security professionals for making their pre-scriptions for cyber security and resilience too 'bullet-point' orientated.

"All too often it comes across as merely a series of tick-boxes on a check-list: don't click on links you don't know; don't plug-in USB sticks from outside; don't send unencrypted files by email… blah, blah blah." Jim has been known to argue with security specialists on panels and in group discussions, accusing them of de-humanising the subject.

"I often have to stop everything and remind the audience that we're talking about *people* here – me and you. People who think they've got it made. People who actually have got it made but, who can unmake it all with a click of a mouse. People at all levels, everyone, but especially people at the top. The truth is the hackers are often cleverer than we are. They use social engineering to manipulate our basic curiosity, desire to help, and – at exec level – turn our sense of pride and entitlement against us. Then, in the blink of an eye, they're in your company looting your most precious information and undermining your reputation. And it hurts. It really does hurt."

FALL-OUT FROM THE SECURITY BREACH

Jim remembers the first few board meetings after the breach. His biggest customers were either shutting down contracts or preparing to. The hack had used Jim's company to get into the systems of one multinational food company, a major pharmaceutical firm and others.

"The motives were hard to discern," remembers Jim, "but we knew that we weren't the primary target pretty quickly. That made it worse. Suddenly, my colleagues on the board were looking at me… well, differently. I wasn't the same Jim Baines. I was the 'careless' Jim Baines."

THE CFO'S EXPERIENCE

Hannah Simmons, CFO of the multinational food company that represented a significant portion of Jim's packaging throughout each year, had an even worse experience.

"I'd created a presentation on my infected laptop, then gave it to Hannah on a USB stick and, contrary to her company's policies, she'd plugged it into her work computer." Jim shakes his head again – he still doesn't believe how simple it all was. "She got roasted by her board. They kept it pretty quiet but she was forced to resign. Then some journalist started to pursue her and the story came out. I feel responsible for what happened to her. She's an old friend – we go way back to when we were at university in London together – and she knows that it wasn't my fault, exactly. But, her loss of reputation probably hurts me more than my own. She lost her position and her job."

REBUILDING C-LEVEL REPUTATIONS

Jim has managed to re-build his reputation somewhat, despite his lingering sense of hurt. By speaking out and being honest about what happened and why, he's begun to turn the situation around. Now, he's a vocal advocate of innovative approaches to changing the behaviours of the whole workforce through engaging and relevant awareness learning, including high-level executives.

"The leadership of any organisation has to know just as much about cyber security as anyone else. In fact, they have to know more. They have to be actively involved in developing and setting policies, they need to proactively oversee that they are being followed and updated. Above all, they need to lead by example".

CYBER SECURITY WISDOM LIES IN COLLECTIVE EXPERIENCE

"After one conference I was approached by this executive who'd studied philosophy at college and he sent me a section out of Socrates – well, Plato's *Apology* to be precise – which relates what Socrates was supposed to have said about being wise." Jim shuffles through some papers and finds the passage in question; it's marked with streaks of yellow highlighter.

"In essence it's this: Socrates talks about the reputation he's gained as the wisest man in the world. The Oracle at Delphi has said he is; so everyone believes that it's true. Socrates knows it isn't but doesn't dare contradict the gods. So, he goes to try and find someone who is wiser than he is. And do you know what he discovers? He probably is the wisest man in the world precisely because he knows he isn't. He knows that he doesn't know it all, and is willing to listen to people who know more than him about their specialist subjects."

Jim's point is that executives have to engage with their IT, security and risk specialists on the basis that each of them knows more than the others about their specific areas, but that none of them know it all and, critically, *everyone* has the responsibility to be aware of the dangers so they can create the right policies and promote the right behaviours to better manage the risks. "If we work together – honestly and openly – then we will be much stronger and more resilient."

LESSONS LEARNED

"The board has to recognise that it might be collectively ignorant when it comes to cyber security. Most members would probably admit that the subject hasn't been high on their own personal agenda, and, probably, it hasn't been discussed very often during meetings." Jim admits that his own board neglected the subject routinely. "We left it to our CIO. It was an IT issue – something that our IT people would handle without much reference to us. I'll admit that, before the breach happened, I probably had only scanned our IT security policy in passing. It was just another piece of paper – in a ream of papers. But, it was the most important one, as it turned out."

Jim advises fellow CEOs to: "bang on about cyber security and keep on doing it until everyone has it in their top three business issues and objectives." Putting cyber security front and centre at board level is a key pillar of any organisation's cyber resilience.

SUMMARY

"Resilience isn't about being 100% secure – no company can achieve that – it's about being able to respond quickly to an attack and bounce back from it. To flex when you're under threat, or you take a hit… and then bounce back to the shape you were in before; only stronger. But it can't be done if there's a missing link – a careless layer of people who don't think the rules apply to them. Especially if that layer is at the highest level of the organisation."

The theme of leadership underpins Jim's focus on reputation. The board can't leave cyber security to the IT team.

"It's not actually their job to man the bastions," says Jim, "that's something everyone has to do. IT facilitates technology and makes sure it works for all the end users, but security is not just about machines, it's about people. So, it's an HR issue, a production, marketing and management issue. It's a people issue, first and foremost."

Jim usually resists the temptation to bullet-point his logic. He disdains lists. "C-level executives get to see too many of them. They go bullet-blind. What they need are stories. Stories like mine." But as he speaks he stabs the air with figurative bullets.

"Start by being honest about how a cyber-breach would hurt you most – your reputation for competence and leadership could be irreparably damaged.

"Once you can picture what it might be like to be blamed for a breach in your organisation… think about how it might happen. Think about how careless you really are each day about security: how you use your smartphone or tablet, how you break the small rules that govern where and how you share files or send emails or use public Wi-Fi … yeah … we all do it.

"Then think about how you can justify your carelessness – your sense that you're entitled to break the rules – to an employee who's been disciplined for doing what you do routinely!

"How can you look them in the eye and reprimand them? You can't.

"Then think about what your other stakeholders might think of you … and how your actions could impact on their lives … and their investment in you – their trust in you.

"It's not pleasant. You know it's going to hurt. It could end your career.

"So, don't do it. Don't feel that you're above the fray. Understand that it can… and probably will… happen to you.

"That gets you back to the beginning. You're a whale because of who and what you are. You're a target, so you need to start acting intelligently if you want to avoid becoming a victim. Follow your own rules. Make sure the rules are good. And make sure everyone else follows them, and that they're coherent and up-to-date.

"Then walk the walk. Or whatever cliché you want to use. Whales are clever creatures, maybe more intelligent than I am! So, act like one. Protect your own species."

I'm tempted to offer 'Save the Whale' as the title of a book he could write about being the victim of cyber crime, but I resist the temptation.

"Warren Buffet put it simply when he said, 'It takes 20 years to build a reputation, and five minutes to ruin it. If you think about that, you'll do things differently.' He's right, of course, only the timeframe has changed now: it doesn't take five minutes anymore. It can take just a nanosecond."

Jim sits back, he stares down at his desk. One of the lines on his phone starts to blink orange, but he ignores it. The scars of his experience are clearly still raw.

"What happened to me can happen to any member of any

board. I'm happy for my story to be out there if it can save someone else the pain of having their reputation, and that of their business, tarnished. All it takes is vigilance, common sense, and some humility."

Read Jim's full story in Whaling for Beginners *published by AXELOS/TSO*

1.3

THE CYBER SECURITY THREAT

Steve Culp and Chris Thompson,
Accenture Finance & Risk Practice for Financial Services

Firms should develop a strategy to cope with the cyber threat emanating from online criminals, hacktivists or nation states looking to destabilise payment and financial systems, such as Russia's alleged 2007 cyber attack against Estonia's financial services ecosystem.[1] The need is most pressing at large scale financial services institutions as many of these sit at the apex of the financial system.

Cyber security has jumped to the top of companies' risk agenda after a number of high profile data breaches, ransom demands, distributed denial of service (DDoS) attacks and other hacks. In an increasingly digitised world, where data resides in the cloud, on mobiles and devices connected to the "Internet of Things" threat vectors are multiplying, threatening firms' operations, customer and bank details and future financial stability.

---

1   Estonia under cyber attack, Hun-CERT. Access at: http://cert. hu/sites/default/files/Estonia_attack2.pdf

In a report on which this chapter is based Accenture and Chartis analysed the benefits of better alignment across operational risk management procedures with cyber security in an enterprise risk management (ERM) framework. The objective for leading firms should be to focus on increasing the resilience of the organization, and despite their best efforts it is highly unlikely that any firm can completely avoid security issues in the digitally-connected world we all operate within.

Cooperation is an essential starting point in the organization— a DDoS attack or data breach impacts people, processes and technology across the business. As well as getting IT systems back up and running financial institutions (FIs) should write to customers and regulators, activate back-up facilities, and compensate any losses. Operational and cyber security employees need lines of communications and a coordinated pre-planned response. Firms should take this opportunity to review their existing risk management processes, departments and responsibilities with respect to cyber security, re-aligning them into an overall operational and ERM strategy with boardroom backing.

THE SCOPE OF THE PROBLEM

You cannot open a paper, or indeed a link, these days without hearing about a new cyber attack. The immediate need for firms to protect themselves is made more pressing by the manner in which regulators retrospectively sanction firms for past breaches.

In September 2015, for instance, the Securities and Exchange Commission (SEC) fined R.T. Jones Capital Equities Management, a St. Louis-based investment adviser, $75,000 for failing to establish the required cyber security policies and procedures in advance of a breach that occurred in July 2013. An unknown hacker gained access to data and compromised the personally identifiable information (PII) of approximately 100,000 individuals, including thousands of the firm's clients, after infiltrating its third-party hosted web server. The attack left R.T. Jones' clients vulnerable to fraud theft and prompted the SEC's action for violating Rule 30(a) of Regulation S-P under the US Securities Act of 1933.[2]

As Marshall S. Sprung, former Co-Chief of the SEC Enforcement Division's Asset Management Unit, said in the ruling: "Firms must adopt written policies to protect their clients' private information and they need to anticipate potential cyber security events and have clear procedures in place rather than waiting to react once a breach occurs."[3] Other examples illustrating the scope of the problem include:

* Interpol and Kaspersky Lab revealed in February 2015[4] that about $1bn had been stolen over a two year period from financial institutions worldwide by a cybercriminal gang comprising members from Russia, Ukraine, and China. The Moscow-based security firm dubbed the criminal gang "Carbanak". The criminal case proves that FIs are just as susceptible to cyber attacks as

---

2   *SEC Charges Investment Adviser With Failing to Adopt Proper Cyber security Policies and Procedures Prior to Breach*, U.S. Securities and Exchange Commission, press release, September 22, 2015. Access at: http:// www.sec.gov/news/ pressrelease/2015-202.html

3   Ibid

4   Cyber bank robbers steal $1bn, says Kaspersky report, February 16, 2015. Access at: http://www.bbc.com/news/ business-31482985

retailers that hold card details or telcos and utilities among others. They are also at the top of the tree for any fraud-related attack.

- The Ponemon Institute LLC has calculated that cyber risk translates to a mean annualized cost, for every company, of $7.7 million.[5]
- In a "2015 Cyber Security Global Survey" conducted by Chartis Research,[6] which questioned 103 risk profes-sionals, 69% of them said they expect their cyber security expenditure to increase the next year by more than 10%.
- The World Economic Forum (WEF) again identified technological risks, in the form of data fraud and cyber attacks, as among the top ten risks in terms of likelihood while critical information infrastructure breakdown was among its top ten risks in terms of impact.[7] The threats are real and growing.

DEFINING THE PROBLEM

Financial institutions (FIs) want to establish controls to manage cyber risk from the top down. However, while FIs are familiar with the basics of firewalls, malware and phishing, they are struggling to connect the technical aspects of cyber security with the people and process risks that operational risk is designed to monitor and control.

---

5   *Forewarned is Forearmed, 2015 Cost of Cyber Crime Study: Global*, October 2015. Access at: http://www8.hp.com/uk/en/ software-solutions/ponemon-cyber-security-report/index.html
6   *Cyber Security Global Survey*, Chartis Research, 2016.
7   *Global Risks 2015*, World Economic Forum. Access at: http:// www3.weforum.org/docs/WEF_Global_ Risks_2015_Report15. pdf

A necessity for establishing control is to first set a good definition of the problem. Many firms produce their own cyber security definition. A common starting point is with the International Organization for Standards' ISO 27k series on IT risk, which includes a cyber security component, under ISO/IEC 27032. It reads as follows:

- Officially, ISO/IEC 27032 addresses "Cyber security" or "Cyberspace security," defined as the "preservation of confidentiality, integrity and availability of information in the Cyberspace."[8]
- In turn, "Cyberspace" is defined as the "complex environment resulting from the interaction of people, software and services on the internet by means of technology devices and networks connected to it, and which does not exist in any physical form."[9]

In the US, the National Institute of Standards and Technology (NIST) can also provide useful definitions and guidelines. Both external frameworks should be examined as part of an early stage project to align operational risk management (ORM) and cyber security procedures.

The main definition problem that FIs encounter is around scope. Broad and narrow definitions of cyber security both have strengths and weaknesses. A broad definition provides wide coverage and lends itself to a cross-silo approach. However, it can lead to confusion over responsibilities and cause significant overlap with other areas like IT security.

---

8   *ISO/IEC 27032:2012 Information Technology – Security techniques – Guidelines for cyber security*, ISO website, online browsing platform. Access at: https://www.iso.org/obp/ui/#iso:std:iso-iec:27032:ed-1:v1:en

9   Ibid

A narrow definition can result in the creation of another tactical risk management silo, which is undesirable. The aim should be to develop an open definition that covers all of the threat vectors, but clearly assigns responsibilities.

Some definitions of cyber security put forward by representatives of international FIs in conversation with Chartis and Accenture appear in Figure 1.4.1.

Figure 1.4.1   Varying Definitions of Cyber security

EXAMPLES OF CYBER SECURITY			
Definition	**Coverage**	**Strengths**	**Weaknesses**
"Protection against services or applications in cyberspace being used for or are the target of a crime, or where cyberspace is the source, tool, target, or place of a crime."	Covering incidents which occur in cyberspace, i.e. online.	Differentiates between local IT issues and online IT.	Doesn't focus on physically-enabled network attacks, such as black boxes.
"Detection, prevention and recovery processes for malicious or deliberate damage, bypass or removal of IT controls."	Covering incidents wherein IT-specific controls are deliberately broken.	Differentiates between IT security and cyber security (by specifying deliberate attacks) and also fraud risks (by specifying IT controls).	Narrow definition; can cause confusion around responsibilities when cross-silo attacks occur such as when a fraud attack is initiated by a phishing malware.

"The body of technologies, processes and practices designed to protect networks, computers, programmes and data from attack, damage or unauthorised access."	Defining cyber security as essentially encompassing the security of all IT processes.	Broad focus, enabling the capture of information from multiple potential silos.	Soft definition; often cannot be distinguished from IT security definitions, such as: "Information security is the set of business processes that protects information assets regardless of how the information is formatted or whether it is being processed, is in transit or is being stored."
"The attempt to subvert information risk controls of the bank for the agenda of the perpetrator."	Defining cyber security as the protection of access to information in an IT system.	Defines information risk controls as a target for perpetrators.	Does not distinguish between technologically enabled and non-technologically enabled attacks.

Source: Chartis Research, based on discussions with financial institutions, August to December 2015

Beyond this, whether definitions are broad or narrow, or principles or rule-based, there appears to be a pressing need to help establish frameworks and move the conversation to the board level. More than definitions, the important factors are responsibility and awareness of what each involved party is doing to help protect the institution.

EXPANDING OPERATIONAL RISK TO INCLUDE CYBER SECURITY

Operational risk is defined by the Basel Committee as: "The risk of direct or indirect loss resulting from inadequate or failed internal processes, people and systems, or from external events."[1]

Cyber attacks from external criminals or internally disgruntled employees can fit this definition. They become a problem only if the processes and people elements in an FI's strategy are not sufficiently developed. If the chief risk officer (CRO) is talking to the chief information security officer (CISO) and both are aware of their specific responsibilities, and how they align with the wider ERM strategy, then a data loss event, DDoS attack or hack needn't be catastrophic. Joining the dots and aligning a strategy is key. The challenge is that cyber security is traditionally managed through its own set of internal controls within IT, which are separate from the duties and processes required for operational risk management or compliance. Bringing cyber security into a common framework is necessary in our view.

In addition, the Basel Committee's 2014 report on operational risk includes cyber attacks as a scenario. This illustrates the nature of the operational risk that can result from cyber security breaches, ranging from continuity to credit and market risk:

"...some banks have developed scenarios related to earthquakes and other catastrophic events such as a cyber-attack to assess not only the operational risk exposures

---

1   *Consultative Document on Operational Risk*, Basel Committee on Banking Supervision, January 2001. Access at: https://www. bis.org/publ/bcbsca07.pdf

(i.e. business continuity, costs, fraud losses, lawsuits, etc.) but also other risks such as credit risk (i.e. increased defaults, devaluations of collateral), market risk and general economic conditions (i.e. lower revenues)."[2]

The expansion of operational risk to include cyber threats is being driven by a number of trends:

1. The rising number and complexity of cyber attacks now represents a real threat to an FI's profitable existence. Reputational damage and regulatory fines await FIs that cannot prove a coordinated response, communication and back-up plan is in place.
2. Boards and senior leadership increasingly recognise that the solution lies beyond the technology layer and in the broader people and processes of the institution.
3. Poor cost-to-income ratios are driving banks to consolidate their silo-based risk management.

The "new normal" of expanded operational risk management (ORM) strategies that align with cyber security, fraud and anti-money laundering (AML) disciplines is illustrated in Figure 1.4.2. For example, cyber security events such as the "Carbanak" $1bn loss from financial institutions worldwide and the Dyre Wolf malware attack against banks[3] show that

---

2   *Review of the Principles for the Sound Management of Operational Risk*, Basel Committee on Banking Supervision, October 6, 2014. Access at: http://www.bis.org/publ/bcbs292.pdf
3   *The Dyre Wolf – Bank Transfer Scam Alert*, National Fraud Intelligence Bureau and City of London Police, April 2015. Access at: http://www.fsb.org.uk/docs/default-source/fsb-org-uk/152/assets/april-2015/the- dyre-wolf---bank-transfer-scam-alert.pdf

phishing, malware, fraud, money laundering and business disruption all go together. A cyber risk response and ORM strategy should be similarly coordinated.

Figure 1.4.2   Operational Risk Management Can Be the Integration Point for Cyber security and Other Risk Management Areas

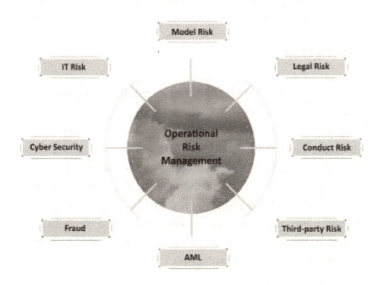

Source: Chartis Research, December 2015

Chartis Research has seen operational frameworks and methodologies expanding into full governance, risk and compliance (GRC) initiatives at FIs. The three lines of defence – inputs such as risk events arising from malware, your monitoring and coping mechanisms and auditing of the strategy – mean that a firm should be able to prove a boardroom-backed governance and risk structure is in place and reinforced by training and testing from the bottom up.

Regulators and partners in the financial supply chain will be reassured by strong managerial oversight and the presence of a cyber risk-aware culture. In addition, the near-immediate dissemination of negative news through social media and the internet has increased the threat of reputational risk. Loss of reputation could lead to a loss of customer and stakeholder trust, loss of revenue, and a higher level of regulatory scrutiny in future, posing a direct threat to executives and the C-suite, who could potentially lose their jobs.

CONCLUSIONS

Bringing together leadership and capabilities across fraud, IT, cyber security and operational risk in this manner can help FIs to "connect the dots" and improve their ERM strategy. Governance, skills, taxonomies and technology should be aligned with the common definition, language and approach delineated at the start of the alignment push between operational and cyber risk. The ability to view cyber security breaches as a risk, with associated probabilities and impacts, help firms focus on striking the right balance between resilience and protection.

The key recommendations from Accenture and Chartis Research include:

- FIs should establish consistent definitions for cyber security. Firms should avoid the potential creation of another risk management silo by using an open definition that also assigns responsibilities in the event of an attack, helping firms to have a consistent view of cyber security across business and IT processes.
- Cyber security should be managed as a risk discipline across the three lines of defence – ownership, oversight

and assurance. This should help firms to align with board-level risk appetite.

- Effective cyber security requires collaboration across silos, knowledge sharing and cooperation between technology and operational risk employees. Each should understand the other's responsibilities. Collaboration between the chief data officer (CDO), CIO, CISO and CRO is very important.
- Coordination between cyber security and operational risk will encourage increased visibility of risks and a communication of cyber security issues at the board level. Boardroom support for the formation of an integrated cyber ORM approach is essential from the top down. Similarly, bottom-up cyber security should be built through a risk-aware culture, including training and periodic testing.
- Alignment between the operational risk and cyber security disciplines should help FIs stay ahead of online criminals, hacktivists and rogue states. A comprehensive pre-planned strategic response will encourage firms to resist the growing cyber threat.

ACKNOWLEDGEMENTS

The authors would like to thank Peyman Mestchian of Chartis Research for his valuable contribution to this paper.

PART TWO

International Action

2.1

INTERNATIONAL COOPERATION FROM THE BANKING SECTOR ONWARDS

Don Randall, Don Randall Associates

PARTNERSHIP AND COLLABORATION

The significant and tragic events of 9/11, the continuing growth of international terrorism and the exponential rise in global cyber related incidents resulting in a current estimated criminal loss of USD$400 billion per annum have created a requirement for two core activities. Firstly, for all organisations to invest in an appropriate security/cyber model which can be either inhouse, outsourced or a hybrid responsibility. Secondly, there is a fundamental need for partnership and collaboration to exist between all legitimate parties in the public and private sector.

On a local, national and international platform the banking community should establish bank-to-bank relationships together with similar relationships with law enforcement and associated bodies, other businesses and their customers. These relationships will require a substantial element of trust in respect of information-sharing and have a robust, speedy and accurate two-way communication vehicle.

CYBER SECURITY STRUCTURE AND STAFFING MODELS

Irrespective of how it is designed or staffed, the security structure requires clear and direct reporting lines to senior management and/or board level. The structure needs to be able to receive and meaningfully interpret streams of information and intelligence. It additionally requires an arterial relationship with both the business lines and those responsible for the information technology infrastructure. An investigative capability is also an essential element of any effective security structure, including the ability to understand the motivation, intention and purpose of any perpetrators and their origin. As an example, these incidents could be motivated by criminal gain, intelligence-gathering, disruption, nuisance, disgruntlement or "just because they can." Equally important is to understand who these "actors" are.

The importance of establishing the correct security structure is emphasised by a 2015 statement from the former City of London Police Commissioner, Adrian Leppard, at the Financial Crimes and Cyber Security Symposium in New York where he announced: "International terrorists will engage in cyber terrorist activity. Leppard said: "We cannot underestimate the determination of international criminals, operating alone or as part of serious organised crime gangs or terrorist organisations, to launch a major strike against our financial centres, particularly in London and New York. It is therefore crucial we take a proactive approach to this threat by putting in place the technical and legal systems that will keep trading platforms secure from malware and prevent companies from being compromised by a rogue employee or weak IT systems."

There are a number of differing security models using varying staffing titles. Historically, the Chief Information Security Officer (CISO) reported to the Chief Information Officer (CIO). However, a recent trend is for the CISO to report directly to the Chief Security Officer (CSO) alongside all other associated security function heads. In 2010, CSO Magazine – together with PWC – conducted a survey which asked who CISOs reported to. Of the 12,847 respondents, only 6.5% described themselves as a CIO (no joint functionality). When CISOs were asked who they reported to, most said the company CEO or board of directors. Less than a quarter of respondents said they reported to the CIO.[4]

WHO SHOULD BE THE HEAD OF SECURITY IN A FINANCIAL ORGANISATION?

It is important to take into account the various models of security and who assumes the responsibility of the head of security. This is dependent upon many factors, including the type of business, the size of the organisation, its locality, its inter-dependencies and its infrastructure. Even when these parameters are met, some organisations choose to accommodate the head of security position within alternative departments/divisions e.g. risk, facilities or central services.

Consideration should also be given to the emerging function of the Chief Risk Officer (CRO). 'Gartner projects that one-third of large enterprises will have a digital risk officer by 2017 and that the role will broadly emerge in

---

4   BRENNER, B (2010) CSO CIOs vs. *CISOs: Pros and cons of an 'adversarial' relationship* [Online] 11th November 2010 Available from: http://www.csoonline.com/article/2126104/ strategic-planning-erm/cios-vs--cisos--pros-and-cons-of-an--adversarial--relationship.html [Accessed: 1st March 2015]

2015. The role will require skills in business knowledge, communication, risk management, privacy and technology. This sounds similar to what has been advocated for the CISO who wishes to secure his or her seat at the corporate strategy table. Make no mistake: the CISO who exhibits dexterity in identifying and mitigating cyber risk will continue to be a key piece of the CISO-CRO dance.'[5]

In September 2013, following the creation of the CISO at the Bank of England, one of the key reporting line decisions was for the CISO to report to the Chief Operating Officer (COO) and Deputy Governor of the Bank and specifically not to the CIO. One of the primary reasons for this decision was the governance factor, thereby creating independence and separation between the CISO responsibilities and those of the CIO.

In considering this discussion, a CISO might be placed at quite a senior level within the organisation, dependent upon its size and nature of its business. Should an organisation have a small footprint of physical assets and employee population, the risks that are associated with these are of less importance and this can be reflected in the level of manager appointed to deal with them; the disciplines in this case could converge under the CISO. For example, at the Central Bank of Switzerland, the head of security role is seen as a senior position and the CISO more junior. At the Bank of England the CISO role is seen as equally important to that of the head of security, notwithstanding the fact that the head of security role encompasses other responsibilities.

In an organisation with a large population, physical

---

5   BURGESS, C (2014) Security Intelligence *CISO vs. CRO: What's the Difference?* [Online] 19th August 2014 Available from: http://securityintelligence.com/ciso-vs-cro-whats-the-difference/#. VPY8jXysWSo [Accessed: 1st March 2015]

assets, and large geographical footprint the breadth of skills, knowledge and abilities required of the security "person in charge" often means that a CSO is required such that the many aspects of security fall under one leader. Information is only one discipline of the multi-faceted nature of security, so a CISO may not be best qualified to deal with breadth.

It is also relevant to point out that there is still some confusion at this time around the title structure; namely, the head of security role is referred to as head of security, chief of security, director of security, head of facilities and security and chief security officer to list some examples. Likewise, some blue chip companies have not created a specific CISO role.

To add to this confusion, the CSO was initially seen as an information technology person, although latterly the role of the CISO has subsumed the combined roles. This creates a clear delineation within information technology between the CIO and the CISO.

It is also interesting to note that the majority of CSOs come from a police, security services or armed services background. Similarly, the CISOs predominantly come from an information technology background. Recently, however, Nationwide and Barclays (and indeed the Bank of England) have appointed non-IT CISOs.

In order to fully evaluate this issue, we need to consider the evolution of the head of security, the CISO and the CSO roles. Consideration must also be given to cultural change, board acceptability and clearly the skillsets of any appointed individual.

Interestingly, the first ever CISO was appointed in 1995 at Citigroup following a Russian malware attack. For some time this role, which was integral to the information technology division and reported to the CIO, was slow to develop. However, in the last 5 years, the CISO role has gathered greater momentum, and is now seen as a key responsibility within any blue chip company.

More and more financial organisations are following the model of independence between the CIO and the CISO, both of whom have separate board room level access. It is not unusual for a CIO to have a board room position.

In conclusion, to enable successful partnership and collaboration within and beyond the financial sector, it is imperative to create a professional security structure thereby enabling the trust and sharing of information to exist.

PARTNERSHIP MODELS

Numerous partnership models exist around the globe. Some countries still have physical, technical and legislative barriers to this activity. This said, all 192 nations within the United Nations family support and endorse the existence and working practices of Interpol.

SISTER BANKS

The sharing of information within the financial sector has been in place for many years on both a local, national and international level. One notable example was the creation in 1996 of a group of financial sector security heads who formed a coalition of international banking organisations with a substantial presence in London. This group, the "Sister Banks" – mirror imaged by its New York equivalent the "Bankers and Brokers" – continues today.

PROJECT GRIFFIN

Following 9/11, the need for partnership and collaboration was firmly established and endorsed internationally. In the United

Kingdom, an opportunity was taken to develop a partnership between UK law enforcement and the private security industry, primarily within the financial sector. The initiative was piloted between September 2003 and April 2004. The pilot encompassed four major international banks based in London and two security companies, together with The City of London and Metropolitan Police forces. This initiative, known as "Project Griffin", was launched in April 2014.

The terrorist attacks on New York and Washington on 11th September 2001 highlighted the evolving nature of the terrorist threat that Western countries would be facing for over a decade and are still combating today. Even before that threat materialised on the streets of London on 7 July 2005, security authorities expected the UK to feature high on the list of appealing targets for Al Qaeda and its affiliates. As a result, attempts were made to encourage and promote greater engagement between the public and private sector around counter-terrorism issues, in the belief that national security was a collective responsibility that could be more effectively pursued by proactively involving a wide range of stakeholders.

In this vein, Project Griffin represented an ambitious initiative aimed at fostering security awareness across the capital's business community through effective and timely information-sharing with law enforcement.

Since its inception, Griffin has expanded significantly and is nowadays viewed as the most effective and successful example of public-private partnership on security issues.

Its stated mission is to "engage, encourage and enable members of the community to work in partnership with the police to deter, detect, and counter terrorist activity and crime," providing an official and direct channel through which the police can share valuable information and provide relevant updates concerning security and crime prevention.

The system has been praised for raising awareness of security and terrorism issues among the business community as well as for facilitating the sharing of valuable intelligence before, during and after a crisis.

Griffin's operational framework includes three main strands:

- *Awareness Days:* Staged locally by participating police forces in order to introduce the project's working concept and help build relationships. Awareness days are used to instruct participants on how to recognise, respond to and report suspicious activity.
- *Conference Bridge Calls:* Through these, participating organisations receive relevant intelligence updates, including information on crime trends and upcoming events that might have implications for public order and safety. In London, such intelligence input is provided by The City of London Police, Metropolitan Police Service, British Transport Police (BTP) and the Counter Terrorist Squad at New Scotland Yard, among others. From their part, private security guards regularly provide law enforcement partners with information on suspicious activity.
- *Emergency Deployments and Cordon Support:* In times of emergency, Griffin guards can be asked to assist police forces in activities such as setting up incident cordons or high-visibility neighbourhood patrolling. Such a deployment is voluntary and subject to agreement by all parties engaged in Griffin.

Although it was originally limited to companies with their own security staff, Griffin has since managed to engage a wider range of commercial businesses across numerous UK towns and cities.

The expertise showcased by private security guards has proved to be greatly beneficial on numerous occasions, including during the 7 July 2005 London bombings when Griffin security officers provided much needed support by carrying out external patrols of premises and by reassuring the communities most directly impacted by the terrorist attack.

As further testament of its success as a valuable and effective information-sharing mechanism, Griffin has been exported to several countries, including Singapore, Australia (currently used in Sydney, Melbourne and Victoria), Canada (where it was utilised during the 2010 Winter Olympics) and the US, and there are currently plans for adopting the program in the Netherlands, France and at Los Angeles Airport. In New York, Griffin was incorporated into the existing Project Shield, an umbrella program designed "to coordinate the efforts of both public and private security activities" for the purpose of protecting the city from terrorist attacks.

CROSS-SECTOR SAFETY AND SECURITY COMMUNICATIONS (CSSC)

In the UK, Griffin has proved to be a critical source of inspiration for a wider and more comprehensive information-sharing platform which was launched in time for, and successfully tested during, the London 2012 Olympic and Paralympic Games. Conceived at the time as a unique partnership between the London Police Services, the Home Office, the Greater London Authority, Transport for London, the London Resilience Team, London First and 23 key industry and business sector groups, CSSC's mission statement was "to provide and facilitate for all London businesses to be safety and security aware before, during and after the Games by improving communication between the public and private sector on security matters, creating a legacy of improved communication and awareness."

CSSC's main strength lies in its truly cross-sector character – currently a total of 34 sector and industry groups are represented – which allows for extensive coverage, as the information is effectively cascaded through various business links, trade organisations and contacts to the wide business community. Currently, such a cascading mechanism ensures CSSC messaging reaches up to 14 million recipients across the UK.

CSSC's other unique feature is its two-way information flow, which aims to provide a real opportunity for businesses to voice their priorities in relation to both security and business continuity issues. In order to do this, a "Hub" has been created to act as the interface between law enforcement and business partners through which real-time information can be fed back, with a view to support authorities and help them optimise their resources. The very idea of creating networks of communication that could be coordinated through the Hub is what allows the message to be cascaded to all connected businesses and potentially the wider local community.

CONCLUSION

Whatever its purpose or motivation, illicit cyber activity continues to attack the financial sector and will undoubtedly do so for many years to come. As financial organisations develop new technologies, then the adversaries will do likewise. Partnership and collaboration is essential to identify who these "actors" are and to create preventative and detection opportunities. The only way to be successful is a multi-agency approach, whereby financial organisations talk to each other, law enforcement agenciess talk to each other and both the financial organisations and law enforcement agencies talk to each other on an international fast-time, accurate and authoritative basis. This collaboration has to find a vehicle whereby suspicions and attempts – as well as actual incidents – are shared on a 24/7 basis. It is similarly essential that the security structure is fit for this purpose.

The examples of the Sister Banks, Project Griffin and CSSC effectively demonstrate the huge necessity for partnership and collaboration and its quantifiable and measurable successes in the prevention, detection and prosecution of security/cyber attacks. The models are easily transferable into any business sector with or without specific areas of focus.

Finally, in the 20 years of these combined models sharing information across a spectrum of business relationships to all categories of recipients across the world, there has never been a single incident of misuse, abuse or inappropriate use of the information provided. A siloed approach to cyber security, avoiding partnership and collaboration, will only allow the perpetrators of these activities to continue and succeed in their goals and missions.

2.2

CYBER SECURITY FRAMEWORK – ADOPTION BY US FINANCIAL SERVICES

Raymond Romero

BACKGROUND

On February 13, 2013, the President of the United States issued Executive Order 13636, Improving Critical Infrastructure Cyber security. The administration recognized the need for critical infrastructure owners and operators to improve how they protect their operations from cyber threats. The administration also recognized that it could not mandate cyber security through legislation. Rather than pursue a top-down approach, the administration concentrated on fostering bottom-up solutions. The order directed the Commerce Department's National Institute of Standards and Technology (NIST) to lead the development of a voluntary ri*align policy, business and technological approaches to address cyber risks.*"[1] The administration also recognised

1   Executive Order 13636 - Improving Critical Infrastructure
Cyber security, 2013

that for a voluntary standard to be widely adopted, it had to be developed in an open and public manner, integrate international standards, and would have to be revised on a regular basis after its initial release. NIST was given one year to develop the framework.

BUILDING THE CYBERSECURITY FRAMEWORK

NIST based the initial draft of the Framework on its continuing work on cyber security standards and guidelines. This work includes the Smart Grid, Identity Management, Federal Information Security Management Act (FISMA), and the Electricity Subsector Cyber security Capability Maturity Model. A copy of the FISMA standards and guidance, as well as the Framework, background materials on its development and implementation tools are freely available on NIST's Computer Security Resource Center website at *csrc.nist.gov*.

In developing the Framework, NIST initially issued a Request for Information (RFI) on February 26, 2013, outlining the properties it believed the Framework should include.

"The Framework should include flexible, extensible, scalable, and technology-independent standards, guidelines, and best practices..."[2]

An outline of the preliminary framework was published on July 1, 2013, and the draft of the preliminary Framework was published on August 28, 2013. NIST released Version 1.0 on February 12, 2014. In addition to soliciting public comment at each stage of the Framework's development, NIST also held a series of workshops – five in total – that brought together stakeholders and facilitated an open dialogue on the contents of the Framework. NIST was

---

2 Developing a Framework To Improve Critical Infrastructure Cyber security, 2013

praised by Industry, Government, Academia, and Standards Organisations for its commitment to an open and collaborative approach.

THE FRAMEWORK

The Framework is comprised of three fundamental components – Core, Implementation Tier and Profile.

The Framework Core (Core) consists of five basic functions that define cyber security at its most basic level. These Core Functions include: Identify, Protect, Detect, Respond and Recover. The functions are defined as follows by the Framework:

- ***Identify*** *– Develop the organisational understanding to manage cyber security risk to systems, assets, data, and capabilities.*
- ***Protect*** *– Develop and implement the appropriate safeguards to ensure delivery of critical infrastructure services.*
- ***Detect*** *– Develop and implement the appropriate activities to identify the occurrence of a cyber security event.*
- ***Respond*** *– Develop and implement the appropriate activities to take action regarding a detected cyber security event.*
- ***Recover*** *– Develop and implement the appropriate activities to maintain plans for resilience and to restore any capabilities or services that were impaired due to a cyber security event.* [3]

Categories subdivide each Function into groups of cyber security outcomes. In turn, Subcategories further

---

3   Framework for Improving Critical Infrastructure Cyber security V1.0, 2014, pp. 8-9

subdivide Categories into specific outcomes of technical and management activities. Informative References tie Subcategories to existing standards, guidelines, and common practices already in use, such as NIST Special Publications, ISACA COBIT 5 standards, ISO/IEC standards and CCS standards. Figure 2.2.1 depicts the Core Functions and Categories with the unique identifiers employed by NIST:[4]

Figure 2.2.1   Core Functions and Categories

Function Unique Identifier	Function	Category Unique Identifier	Category
ID	Identify	ID.AM	Asset Management
		ID.BE	Business Environment
		ID.GV	Governance
		ID.RA	Risk Assessment
		ID.RM	Risk Management Strategy
PR	Protect	PR.AC	Access Control
		PR.AT	Awareness and Training
		PR.DS	Data Security
		PR.IP	Information Protection Processes and Procedures
		PR.MA	Maintenance
		PR.PT	Protective Technology
DE	Detect	DE.AE	Anomalies and Events
		DE.CM	Security Continuous Monitoring
		DE.DP	Detection Processes
RS	Respond	RS.RP	Response Planning
		RS.CO	Communications
		RS.AN	Analysis
		RS.MI	Mitigation
		RS.IM	Improvements
RC	Recover	RC.RP	Recovery Planning
		RC.IM	Improvements
		RC.CO	Communications

---

4   Framework for Improving Critical Infrastructure Cyber security V1.0, 2014, p. 19

FRAMEWORK IMPLEMENTATION TIERS

There are four tiers defined by the Framework: Partial, Risk-Informed, Repeatable, and Adaptive. Under the framework an organisation needs to performs a self-assessment of their Risk Management Processes, Integrated Risk Management Program and External Participation and take into account *"current risk management practices, threat environment, legal and regulatory requirements, business/mission objectives and organisational constraints".*[5] This process facilitates a rigorous self-assessment at a point in time; it helps an organization define how it views cyber security and identify the processes in place to manage risk. The results of this process also serves as an input into Profile process, discussed below.

FRAMEWORK PROFILE

The Framework Profile (Profile) is the *"alignment of the Functions, Categories, and Subcategories with the business requirements, risk tolerance and the resources of the organization."*[6] The Current Profile defines the current state while the Target Profile defines the desired cyber security risk management objectives. Once the current and desired states are defined, a roadmap can be developed that identifies specific actions that must be taken to improve cyber security – which could include the reduction of risks, better alignment with the organisation's business needs and sector goals, legal and regulatory mandates as well

---

5   Framework for Improving Critical Infrastructure Cyber security V1.0, 2014, p. 5

6   Framework for Improving Critical Infrastructure Cyber security V1.0, 2014, p. 5

the adoption of industry best practices. Once a roadmap has been developed, a plan of actions can be formulated that defines how the Target Profile can be achieved. A risk-based approach is recommended – management can make rational choices between multiple alternatives on how best to improve an organisation's Profile.

FRAMEWORK IMPLEMENTATION

The Framework proposes a multi-tiered risk management process that encompasses three Levels: Executive Level, Business/Process Level and the Implementation/Operations Level. It is expected that mission priorities, available resources and risk tolerance decisions are made at the Executive Level and are communicated to the Business/Process level. The Business/ Process level, in turn, would use this information as input into its risk management process. Moreover, the Business/ Process level would collaborate with the Implementation/ Operations level to communicate business needs, define the Current Profile, formulate a Target Profile and develop an implementation plan to address these gaps. The Implementation/Operations level would be expected to monitor and communicate its progress in implementing the Target Profile back to the Business/Process level. The Business/Process level, in turn, would assess the impact and communicate results to the Executive Level. As a repeatable process, it can be followed at the pace selected by the organisation to identify and prioritise opportunities for improving cyber security.

The Framework outlines the following seven steps:

• ***Step 1: Prioritise and Scope.*** Define priorities and scope of the cyber security programme.

- ***Step 2: Orient.*** Determine what systems and assets are in scope, define regulatory requirements, and articulate overall risk approach and associated threats and vulnerabilities.
- ***Step 3: Create a Current Profile.*** Identify the Category and Subcategory outcomes that are currently achieved.
- ***Step 4: Conduct a Risk Assessment.*** Assess the likelihood and impact of various cyber security events.
- ***Step 5: Create a Target Profile.*** Identify the Category and Subcategory outcomes the organization would like to improve or achieve. This process may also include the addition of Category and Subcategory outcomes not in the Framework but deemed important by the organisation or which are mandated by regulations.
- ***Step 6: Determine, Analyse, and Prioritise Gaps.*** Comparison of the Current Profile and the Target Profile to identify gaps. Plans of action can then be developed that address the gaps and identify priorities and resource requirements.
- ***Step 7: Implement Action Plan.*** The organisation determines which actions to take in regards to the gaps, if any, identified in the previous step. It then monitors its current cyber security practices against the Target Profile.[7]

Voluntary Critical Infrastructure Cybersecurity Program

Presidential Policy Directive 21 (PPD21): Critical Infrastructure Security and Resilience was issued on February 12, 2013 and superseded Homeland Security Presidential Directive – 7. PPD21 identifies 16 critical infrastructure sectors and assigns coordination responsibilities of each sector to

---

7   Framework for Improving Critical Infrastructure Cyber security V1.0, 2014, pp. 14-15

a Sector-Specific Agency.[8] The Department of Treasury is the sector-specific agency responsible for coordinating the Financial Services sector. Critical infrastructure protection is also coordinated through a private-sector led council and a government-led committee. The private-sector lead council is the Financial Services Sector Coordinating Council for Critical Infrastructure Protection and Homeland Security (FSSCC) and the government-led committee is the Financial and Banking Information Infrastructure Committee (FBIIC). Also, key stakeholders include the Private Sector Financial Services Information Sharing and Analysis Center (FS-ISAC) and the Financial Regulators (Financial and Banking Information Infrastructure Committee).

Section 8 of Executive Order 13636 directs the Sector-Specific Agencies to establish Voluntary Programs supporting the adoption of the Framework by critical infrastructure owners and operators. Each Sector-Specific Agency is expected to coordinate with their Sector Coordinating Councils to develop implementation guidance and supplement the Framework as required to address sector-specific risks.[9]

---

8 PPD21 defines the following critical infrastructure sectors: Chemical, Commercial Facilities, Communications, Critical Manufacturing, Dams, Defense Industrial Base, Emergency Services, Energy, Financial Services, Food and Agriculture, Government Facilities, Healthcare and Public Health, Information Technology, Nuclear Reactors, Materials, and Waste, Transportation Systems, and Water and Wastewater Systems.
9 Executive Order 13636 - Improving Critical Infrastructure Cyber security, 2013

FINANCIAL SERVICES ADOPTION OF FRAMEWORK

As illustrated in Figure 2.2.2, The Federal Financial Institutions Examination Council (FFIEC) is an interagency regulatory body consisting of the Federal Reserve Board (FRB), the Federal Deposit Insurance Corporation (FDIC), the National Credit Union Administration (NCUA), the Office of Comptroller of the Currency (OCC), the Consumer Financial Protection Bureau (CFPB) and the State Liaison Committee (SLC).[10]

Figure 2.2.2   Structure of The Federal Institutions Examination Council

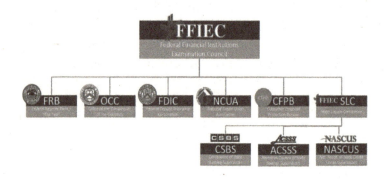

The FFIEC is "*empowered to prescribe uniform principles, standards, and report forms to promote uniformity in the supervision of financial institutions*".[11] The FFIEC's Federal

---

10   Miller, 2015
11   About the FFIEC, n.d.

Financial Institutions Examination Council has developed comprehensive guidance which is communicated through a series of booklets that comprise the Information Technology Examination Handbook (Handbook) – presently there are 11 IT Booklets that contain a wide range of IT controls and processes. On June 30, 2015, the FFIEC released the Cyber security Assessment Tool (Assessment Tool) that financial institutions can use to identify cyber risks and assess their cyber security preparedness. The principles included in the Assessment Tool correspond to the Framework and the FFIEC's existing guidance. Both the Handbook and Assessment Tool are available on FFIEC's website at *www. ffiec.gov*.[12]

ASSESSMENT PROCESS

In developing the Assessment Tool, the FFIEC incorporated controls outlined in the Handbook as well as concepts from other industry standards. The Assessment Tool contains a total of 494 controls compared to the 98 controls that comprise the Framework. A cross-map of the Assessment Tool to the Framework is available on the FFIEC's website.[13]

Inherent Risk Profile

The FFIEC cyber security assessment process consists of two parts: Inherent Risk Profile and Cyber security Maturity. When both are completed, an institution can assess whether its inherent risk and preparedness are effectively aligned.

The inherent risk profile process takes into account

---

12   About the FFIEC, n.d.

13   (Appendix B: Mapping Cyber security Assessment Tool to NIST Cyber security Framework, 2015)

Technology and Connection Types, Delivery Channels, Online/Mobile Products and Technology Services, Organisational Characteristics and External Threats. The inherent risk profile *"helps management determine exposure to risk that the institution's activities, services, and products individually and collectively pose to the institution."*[14] Five risk levels are defined: Least, Minimal, Moderate, Significant and Most.

Cyber security Maturity

The maturity process is intended to help management measure an institution's level of risk and corresponding controls. The maturity model consists of five domains:

* Cyber Risk Management and Oversight
* Threat Intelligence and Collaboration
* Cyber security Controls
* External Dependency Management
* Cyber Incident Management and Resilience

"Within each domain are assessment factors and contributing components. Under each component, there are declarative statements describing an activity that supports the assessment factor at that level of maturity." Figure 2.2.3 below depicts the five domains and associated assessment factors.[15]

---

14   FFIEC Assessment Tool - Overview for Chief Executive Officers and Boards of Directors, 2015, p. 2
15   FFIEC Assessment Tool - Overview for Chief Executive Officers and Boards of Directors, 2015, p. 3

Figure 2.2.3 Domains and Associated Factors

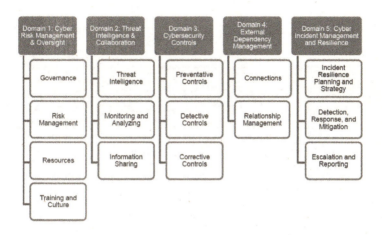

Completing the Cyber security Maturity Profile

For each domain and maturity level, there is a set of declarative statements. Declarative statements are organised into Components, which are groups of similar declarative statements. *"All declarative statements in each maturity level and previous levels must be attained and sustained to achieve that domain's maturity level."* Listed below in Figure 2.2.4 is an example of an assessment for a Domain and associated declarative statements.[16]

---

16 FFIEC Assessment Tool - Overview for Chief Executive Officers and Boards of Directors, 2015, p. 8

Figure 2.2.4 Assessment for a Domain and Associated Declarative Statements

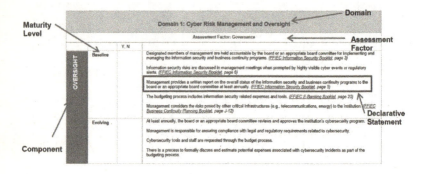

If the institution's maturity level is assessed as not being appropriate in relation to the inherent risk profile, then management must either reduce the inherent risk or develop a plan to improve the maturity level as identified in Figure 2.2.5. The improvement process would include determining a target maturity level, conducting a gap analysis, developing a plan of action, implementing the changes and reevaluating results.[1]

---

1 FFIEC Assessment Tool - Overview for Chief Executive Officers and Boards of Directors, 2015, p. 9

Figure 2.2.5   Assessment of Risk/Maturity Levels

Risk/Maturity Relationship		Inherent Risk Levels				
		Least	Minimal	Moderate	Significant	Most
Cybersecurity Maturity Level for Each Domain	Innovative				▓	▓
	Advanced			▓		
	Intermediate		▓	▓		▓
	Evolving				▓	
	Baseline			▓		

ROLE OF BOARD OF DIRECTORS AND CHIEF EXECUTIVE OFFICER

Given the impact cyber attacks can have on institutions' operations, boards of directors play an increased role in cyber-risk management. This role is consistent with the general obligation to protect corporate assets, including confidential and proprietary information, reputation and goodwill. The FFIEC provides guidance in its Information Technology Handbook on Management, updated in 2015. The FFIEC's guidance stresses:

"The board should approve the IT strategic plan, information security program, and other IT-related policies." The CEO is responsible for *"the development and implementation of the IT strategy to support the institution's business strategy in line with its risk appetite."*[2]

The CEO must, therefore, develop a plan to conduct the cyber security assessment and review and approve plans to address risk management and control weaknesses.

The FFIEC Framework is an iterative risk management process. It facilitates a regular dialog between a board and executive management on how the institution is addressing

---

2   FFIEC IT Examination Handbook - Management, n.d., p. 4

cyber risks. With each iteration, the institution can track how risk profiles and cyber security maturity ratings have improved with the completion of action plans initiated as a result of the assessment process.

FRAMEWORK 2.0

In December 2015, NIST issued an RFI soliciting feedback regarding use of the Framework, proposed updates and governance. In addition to the RFI, NIST held a workshop in April 2016 to solicit input. NIST received 105 responses to the RFI and approximately 800 individuals participated in the workshop. In June 2016, NIST published the *Cyber security Framework Feedback – What we learned and Next Steps* (NIST Website). Based on the feedback received, NIST plans to initially focus on clarifying and refining the Framework. They are targeting early 2017 to issue a draft of the update. This update will focus on *"updating the informative references, clarifying guidance for implementation tiers, placement of cyber threat intelligence in the Core, and guidance for applying the Framework for supply chain risk management."*[3]

NIST also plans to continue its outreach to small and midsized business through the NIST SMB Outreach Program, which provides general cyber security awareness and training and provides 20+ regional training awareness programs seminars each year. NIST's SMB Outreach Program intends to focus on helping SMBs more effectively manage cyber security risks using the Framework.[4]

---

3   Cyber security Framework Feedback - What We Heard and Next Steps, 2016, p. 8

4   Cyber security Framework Feedback - What We Heard and Next Steps, 2016, p. 9

SUMMARY

Executive Order 13636, while aimed at U.S. critical infra-structure enterprises, represents an important step in addressing the cyber security challenge faced by all enterprises. The resulting Cyber security Framework developed by NIST provides a logical and comprehensive approach that can be adopted by any enterprise to effectively addressing cyber threats. It brings together existing standards in an iterative risk management framework that is repeatable and can be followed by any enterprise irrespective of size and complexity. Organisations that adopt the Framework or derivatives, such as the FFIEC Assessment Tool, quickly realise that cyber security is not a one-time task with a discreet start and end. Enterprises realize that addressing cyber security risks is a continuous management process that requires engagement by management and staff at all levels in an organisation. Moreover, executive management, in collaboration with their Board of Directors, set the tone regarding the level of risk an enterprise accepts and the level of investment made to address cyber risks. While bad actors will continue to attack enterprises, the NIST framework will help organisations defend their assets against attack. It is the author's optimistic opinion that the Framework will have a lasting positive impact, domestic and internationally, improving the due standard of care followed by enterprise of all sizes.

2.3

CYBER SECURITY SUPPORT SERVICES FOR UK PUBLIC AND PRIVATE SECTORS

Jonathan Reuvid, Legend Business Books

THE ANATOMY OF GOVERNMENT SPONSORED SERVICES

The awareness and involvement of national governments in cyber security risk management in terms of shared intelligence, avoidance, mitigation and counter action has accelerated since the 1990s and continues to grow as threats multiply.

Driven by terrorist threats to national security, defence and the financial sector, the most notable triggers for increased cooperation and collective responsibility with private industry have been the 11 September 2001 and 7 July 2005 terrorist attacks in New York and London and, more recently, significant commercial incidents such as the invasion of internet service providers. In the last two years terrorist attacks across Europe, in particular in France, Germany and Turkey have heightened the need for advanced cyber intelligence.

In the UK the benefits of sophisticated cyber protection

techniques and processes have been cascaded down from the defence and financial sectors to private industry through the formation and operation of collaborative initiatives under Cabinet Office direction. In chapter 2.1 Don Randall describes the initiatives taken by international banking organisations in response to 9/11 and the evolution of the Project Griffin partnership between UK law enforcement agencies and the private security industry aimed primarily at the London-based financial sector. This chapter outlines the government initiated services available to private industry in general. For more detailed information, readers are referred to the websites identified in the text.

For those addressing the availability of free support services in cyber security the acronyms of the organisations and their origins can be confusing. The following are the key players:

THE NATIONAL CYBER SECURITY CENTRE (NCSC)

Established in 2016, NCSC reports to GCHQ, drawing on its world-class expertise and is tasked to work with industry, academia and international partners to protect the UK against cyber attacks. The newly formed NCSC produces tailored advice and guidance for identified sectors, initially those which constitute the UK's critical national infrastructure and those of strategic or economic significance or which are important to the delivery of key public services.

Working with other government departments including the Home Office and Department for Culture Media and Sport (DCMS) as well as the Cabinet Office, the NCSC also supports the national campaign to grow the UK's cyber security capability and capacity.

To fulfil its mandate of putting strong and innovative approaches in place in order to consolidate its position as a world leader in cyber security, NCSC is in the process of bringing together the established capabilities of CESG, the information security arm of GCHQ, the Centre for the Protection of National Infrastructure, CERT-UK and the Centre for Cyber Assessment. The joined up organisation will greatly simplify the current arrangements to the benefit of the diverse users of these services. The prospectus for NCSC may be downloaded from *https://www.gov.uk/.../5254/ncsc_ prospectus_final_version_1_0.pdf*

The UK National Computer Emergency Response Team (CERT-UK)

Established during 2013, CERT-UK takes the lead in coordinating the management of national cyber security incidents and acts as the central contact point for the UK with its international counterparts. It works closely with industry, government and academia to increase cyber resilience. By sharing information with partners' computer emergency teams and collaborating with national CERTs worldwide, understanding of the cyber threat is further enhanced.

The advice provided by CERT-UK takes the form of access free website content, complementary to services provided for the US (*Cert.org* and *http://www.us-cert.gov/*), Australia (*AusCERT.org.au*), Canada (*cancert.ca*) and Poland (*cert.pl*)

The work of CERT-UK will be transferring to the NCSC in October 2016 as the organisation will not be operational from that point.

The Cybersecurity Information Sharing Partnership (CiSP)

CiSP was launched in March 2014, a joint initiative between industry and the government to provide a catalyst for collaboration in sharing cyber threat and vulnerability information. The service, free to members through network monitoring reports, is administered and delivered by CERT-UK and will continue operating under the aegis of NCSC from October this year. The details of CiSP services and how to apply for membership online may be found at time of writing on *https.//www.cert.gov.uk/cisp/*

ROLES AND GOALS

The NCSC Remit

The original mandate of the NCSC was based on four key objectives:

- To understand the cyber security environment, share knowledge and use that expertise to identify and address systemic vulnerabilities;
- To reduce risks to the UK by working with public and private sector organisations to improve their cyber security;
- To respond to cyber security incidents to reduce the harm they cause in the UK;
- To nurture and grow the national cyber security capability and provide leadership on critical national cyber security issues.

Up to October 2016, NCSC engagement with industry beyond the sectors forming the critical national infrastructure of the UK and of strategic or economic importance focused on those delivering public services, such as energy, telecoms and the finance sector. Now, with the absorption of CESG and CERT-UK, the interface between NCSC as the umbrella organisation for all the services provided by these agencies is broadened through CiSP to include all sectors of industry and SMEs.

The overriding mission of the NCSC is to help ensure that citizens as well as both public and private organisations and the critical national infrastructure are safer online. In doing so, it will bring together the UK's cyber expertise by adopting structured consultation with the private sector to transform how the UK tackles cyber security issues. One of its first tasks will be to work with the Bank of England, which has been at the forefront of confronting the cyber security challenge, to produce advice for the financial sector to manage cyber security more effectively.

In the face of ever-growing threats of cyber attack from serious crime gangs and hacking groups as well as terrorists and foreign states, NCSC will be the authoritative voice on information security in the UK. As Robert Hannington, Director GCHQ, commented at its launch: "Given the industrialscale theft of intellectual property from our companies and universities, as well as the numerous phishing and malware scams that waste time and money, the NCSC shows that the UK is focusing its efforts to combat the threats that exist online. The NCSC will continue the outstanding work by all of the existing organisations to protect national security and our economic success."

Based in London from October, the NCSC is being led by Ciaran Martin, formerly Director General Cyber at GCHQ and supported by Dr. Ian Levy who also moves from BGCHQ to join the new organisation as Technical Director. Contact: *opendoor@ncsc.gov.uk*

CiSP SERVICES

For organisations of all sizes across sectors, the availability of free CiSP membership is a valuable asset. CiSP members from across sectors and organisations are empowered to exchange cyber threat information in real time, in a secure and dynamic environment and within an operating framework that protects the confidentiality of shared information. Other benefits of membership are best practice guides and the issue of regular advice and guidance on cyber issues with the objective of encouraging the sharing of information and best practice within the CiSP community.

CiSP members are offered a network monitoring report detailing malicious activity based on a number of network abuse feeds received and processed. Members need to provide details of their internet facing IT infrastructure. Their network details are stored securely and used for comparison against the malicious events that are received 24 hours a day. If any part of a member's infrastructure is found to relate to any of this activity an email notification will be sent to the CiSP member within 60 seconds. Depending on an organisation's needs and scale of the network, weekly reports can also be scheduled.

Members will be warned about:

- Infected hosts (e.g. bots communicating with sinkholes);
- Compromised hosts that are serving malware;
- Attacking IPs (hosts inside a network observed conducting attacks);
- Sources of spam and phishing;
- Indicators derived from malware analysis;
- Botnet infrastructure (e.g. command and control);
- Web server defacements;
- Perceived vulnerable network services.

The service is supplementary to normal intrusion detection systems and other security systems and should not be treated as an alternative.

Members receive enriched cyber threat and vulnerability information from the "Fusion Cell", a team of joint industry and government analysts who examine and feed back cyber information from diverse data sources, which ultimately adds value to CiSP members and helps them at all levels of cyber maturity. The Fusion Cell will also help members to connect with fellow industry partners and recommend groups for participation.

Full risk assessment of CiSP has been made and suitable controls and measures have been put in place. The CiSP platform is scanned regularly for vulnerabilities and is penetration tested. CiSP is itself hosted in a secure UK datacentre in an environment built to CESG best practices and IL3 standards.

CiSP Membership

Registered membership of CiSP is open to:

- UK registered companies or other legal entities responsible for the administration of an electronics network in the UK;
- Applicants sponsored by either a government department, an existing CiSP member or trade body or association.

Organisations and individuals applying for membership require a sponsor: either a member of an Industry Information Exchange or a trusted member as authorised by NCSC, to testify that the new applicant is genuine and has a bona fide reason for joining CiSP. An application may be completed within 5 minutes and, if successful, the applicant will receive an invitation to join within 5 days. Once organisation membership is approved, staff members may use the individual application form to start using CiSP services.

The value of collaboration as participating members of CiSP has been recognised by industry, particularly larger organisations, since its March 2013 launch and by May 2016 the growing membership exceeded 2,225 organisations and 6,150 individuals.

THE CHALLENGE FOR SMES

The Information Handling Scheme offers CiSP members access to the information that other members have posted and opted to share. For SMEs who value the experience of other SMEs in the same field or industry sector, the amount of pertinent information available depends upon how many of their peer enterprises have joined CiSP as fully participating members. Therefore, the value of the service is to some degree proportionate to the scale of membership taken up by other SMEs.

And herein lies the challenge. According to a recent report by Juniper Research summarised in the 19 September 2016 edition of Computer Weekly, almost 74% of UK small and medium-size enterprises (SMEs) think they are safe from cyber attack although half of them admitted to having suffered a data breach. With this outlook they are hardly a promising community for membership recruitment.

Nevertheless, 50% of the small businesses surveyed had suffered a data breach of some kind, two-thirds in the previous 12 months. In spite of that, 86% of SMEs surveyed thought that they were doing enough to counter the effects of other cyber attacks. According to Windsor Holden, Juniper Research's head of forecasting and consultancy: "Our study shows that businesses believe they are far more secure than they really are" – although a cyber attack could cost a company millions of pounds in lost reputation, data, time and customers. One aspect of this complacency is that 27% of respondents thought that they were safe from attack because they were small and of no interest to criminals.

Almost 90% of SMEs surveyed claimed that they had

a plan in place for responding to a data breach. However, there is a degree of naivety about the significance of data breaches. The survey revealed that while 69% would contact someone immediately after discovering a breach, 18% would wait until the next working day if the incident did not seem to be serious.

RESPONSIBILITY FOR CYBERSECURITY

Board involvement is critical because today all businesses should view occurrence of the unexpected as commonplace. However, 33% of SMEs in the Juniper Research survey considered that their IT departments were solely responsible for managing cyber security threats and only 25% had a board level dedicated security executive.

The Juniper research report is not wholly negative; some SMEs are taking cyber security seriously. Some 48% have adopted secure practice guidelines and 47% give secure practice induction briefings to staff with 25% having a dedicated security executive. Penetrations tests to estimate the likelihood of an attack are carried out by 27% and emails are monitored for phishing attempts by 31% of those surveyed.

The widely reported data breach suffered by TalkTalk in October 2015, which caused the exposure of the personal details of 155,000 customers, is a cautionary tale. Speaking after the event, Kristine Olson-Chapman, general manager at TalkTalk Business, said, "For us, cyber security is no longer just a technology issue; it's a business issue for the whole company. Any business that has ever had a cyber attack will tell you they never expected it, even with all the processes in place. Businesses need to ask themselves what they need to do now to plan and prepare."

Although TalkTalk does not fall within the SME

classification, its experience should be taken as a call to arms for smaller businesses and organisations. The more who join CiSP and exchange information, the greater the benefits of others' cyber security experience to them and their peer groups. For 2017 an expansion in CiSP membership to 20,000 seems a modest target.

NOTES

1. *Readers of this chapter, on publication, will find that the integration of CESG and CertUK services under the NCSC is already in place.*
2. *Much of the material for this chapter was drawn from the several websites of GCHQ and CERT-UK whose permission is acknowledged with thanks.*
3. *Source material, also gratefully acknowledged, was derived from Computer Weekly extracts from the Juniper Research survey of SMEs.*

2.4

EU AND UK CYBER SECURITY DEVELOPMENTS

Ross McKean, Partner, DLA Piper UK

INTRODUCTION

ESTIMATED COSTS OF CYBER CRIME AND CYBER ESPIONAGE

With the annual cost of cyber crime and cyber espionage to the world economy estimated at up to US$575 billion[1] and a series of high profile cyber attacks over the last few years, there has been sustained pressure on legislators to toughen cyber laws.

DEFINING CYBER LAW

Cyber law is not a term of art. It is generally understood to include laws and regulations relating to cyber security (both physical and virtual security), data breach, threat intelligence sharing and incident response and to related regulatory and trade body guidance and enforcement actions.

---

1   Centre for Strategic and International Studies, *Net Losses: Estimating the Global Cost of Cybercrime*, June 2014

TRENDS IN EU CYBER LAW

There are three clear trends emerging from EU and Member State cyber laws:

- a broad legal standard of care to maintain "appropriate" security standards, informed by the current state of the art and by the nature of the data requiring protection;
- greater transparency requirements including obligations to notify data breaches to regulators and in some cases to affected individuals within very short timescales; and
- much tougher sanctions for non-compliance and a greater risk of follow-on private claims.

NEW EU CYBER LAWS

The cyber security strategy for the European Union[1] and the European agenda on security[2] provide an overall framework for the numerous EU initiatives to improve cyber security and tackle cyber crime. This remains a key priority for the EU institutions which have repeatedly stated that the digital economy within the single market depends on trust in secure information networks and systems.

THE GENERAL DATA PROTECTION REGULATION

On 27 April 2016, the General Data Protection Regulation was published in the Official Journal of the European Union

---

1   See https://ec.europa.eu/digital-single-market/en/news/communication-cybersecurity-strategy-european-union-%E2%80%93-open-safe-and-secure-cyberspace or Chapter 1.1 for further information

2   See http://europa.eu/rapid/press-release_IP-15-4865_en.htm

("GDPR").[3] It will apply throughout the European Union, without the need for any implementing legislation, from 25 May 2018. GDPR will replace the current suite of Member State laws implementing the Data Protection Directive 95/46/EC.

More personal data caught within the regulated perimeter

The switch from analogue to digital technologies, ever more powerful consumer devices and rapid technological advances in monetising big data have all driven a huge increase in the amount of information generated and collected by organisations.

Much of this information includes personal data, which is very broadly defined under GDPR including "*any information relating to an identified or identifiable natural person*". A low bar is set for "*identifiable*". If anyone can identify a natural person from a data set using "*all means likely to be used*" then the data is personal data. A name is not necessary; any identifier will do, such as an IP address or other identification number.

Revenue based fines

Failure to comply with security and data breach obligations can lead to fines of up to 10 million Euros or in the case of an undertaking up to 2% of total worldwide turnover of the preceding year, whichever is higher.[4]

Even higher fines of up to 20 million Euros or in the case of an undertaking up to 4% of total worldwide turnover of the preceding year, whichever is higher, are reserved

---

3   Regulation (EU) 2016/679

4   GDPR, Article 83(4)

for failure to comply with the core GDPR principles, data subject rights, international transfer restrictions and certain other infringements.[5] As a serious data breach often leads to a regulatory investigation revealing other areas of non-compliance, organisations may well be exposed to these higher fines when notifying breaches.

Regulators enjoy broad investigative and corrective powers

Supervisory authorities also enjoy wide investigative and corrective powers including the right to undertake on-site audits, to issue public warnings and reprimands and to require organisations to carry out specific remedial measures.[6]

Increased risk of follow-on private claims by affected individuals

GDPR makes it considerably easier for individuals to bring private claims against organisations. There is no requirement to prove financial loss; distress is sufficient.[7] Individuals also have the right to mandate a consumer protection body to exercise rights on their behalf.[8]

Security requirements

Article 32 requires controllers and processors, taking into account the state of the art, the costs of implementation and

---

5   GDPR, Article 83(5)

6   GDPR, Article 58

7   There is a right to claim compensation for "material or non-material damage" - GDPR, Article 82(1)

8   GDPR, Article 80

the nature, scope, context and purposes of processing as well as the risk of varying likelihood and severity for the rights and freedoms of natural persons, to implement "*appropriate technical and organisational measures to ensure a level of security appropriate to the risk*". Examples of specific measures are set out, including the pseudonymisation and encryption of personal data; the ability to ensure the ongoing confidentiality, integrity, availability and resilience of processing systems and services; the ability to restore availability, and "*a process for regularly testing, assessing and evaluating the effectiveness of technical and organisational measures for ensuring the security of the processing*".

Data breach notification requirements

With the exception of certain sector focussed laws[9] and individual Member State laws, there is currently no European wide law requiring notification of data breaches.

One of the most profound changes to be introduced by GDPR is a universal requirement to notify data breaches. Similar requirements under many US State laws have completely transformed the way that US organisations respond to data breaches and have resulted in large fines, extensive litigation, various Senate hearings and numerous C-suite resignations.

Under GDPR, controllers are required "*without undue delay, and where feasible, not later than 72 hours after having become aware of it, [to] notify the ... breach to the supervisory authority*".[10] When the breach is likely to result in a high risk to the rights and freedoms of individuals the controller is also

---

9   For example, providers of publicly available electronic communications services are required to notify data breaches under the e-Privacy Directive 2002/58/EC (as amended)

10   GDPR, Articles 33 and 34

required to notify them *"without undue delay"*. Processors (e.g. suppliers) are required to notify the controller without undue delay having become aware of the breach.

The notification to the regulator must include where possible the categories and approximate numbers of individuals and records concerned, the name of the organisation's Data Protection Officer or other contact, the likely consequences of the breach and the measures taken to mitigate harm.

Notification will therefore become the norm under GDPR and organisations have a great deal of work to do to build the data breach notification infrastructure to enable compliance with these strict new requirements.

There is much more to GDPR than security and data breach notification and although beyond the scope of this book, organisations have a great deal to do before GDPR engages in May 2018.

THE NETWORK AND INFORMATION SECURITY DIRECTIVE

Entry into force

On 19 July 2016, the Network and Information Security Directive ("NISD") was published in the Official Journal of the European Union.[11] Unlike GDPR, which will apply automatically across Europe from 25 May 2018, NISD will have to be implemented into law by each Member State in domestic legislation by 10 May 2018.

On the one hand, NISD is narrower in application than GDPR, applying only to Member States, essential services operators, and digital services providers. On the other hand, NISD is broader than GDPR as it applies to information

---

11   Directive 2016/1148

security whatever the underlying information is, whether it includes personal data or not.

NISD is an important building block in the development of effective cooperation, security and defence against cyber attacks within the European Union. The principal aim of NISD is to *"lay down measures with a view to establishing a high common level of security of network and information systems within the Union so as to improve the functioning of the internal market"*.[12]

To do this, NISD imposes obligations directly on Member States as well as requiring Member States to implement in national laws certain obligations on operators of essential services and on digital service providers.

Obligations on Member States

NISD requires each Member State[13]:

- to adopt a national strategy on the security of network and information systems;
- to designate a competent authority to implement and enforce NISD;
- to create Computer Security Incident Response Teams (CSIRTs) to respond to incidents and manage risks; and
- to identify all operators of essential services with an establishment in the Member State by 9 November 2018. These will include public or private entities performing certain functions in the energy, transport, banking, financial market infrastructures, health, water and digital infrastructure sectors and meeting the following criteria: (a) they provide a service essential for the maintenance of

---

12   NISD, Article 1(1)

13   NISD, Articles 1(2) and 5(1)

critical societal and/or economic activities; (b) the provision of that service depends on network and information systems; and (c) an incident would have significant disruptive effects on the provision of that service.[14]

NISD also creates a cooperation group to support and facilitate cooperation and information exchange among Member States and creates a network of national CSIRTs to promote swift coordinated responses to incidents and information sharing.

Obligations to be imposed on operators of essential services

Member States are required to ensure that operators of essential services[15]:

- manage risk – by taking appropriate and proportionate technical and organisational measures having regard to the state of the art and the risk posed;
- minimise the impact of incidents with a view to ensuring service continuity – by taking appropriate measures to prevent and minimise the impact of incidents affecting the security of network and information systems used to provide essential services; and
- notify, "without undue delay" the competent authority in their Member State or the CSIRT of incidents having a significant impact on the continuity of essential services they provide. Where public awareness is necessary in order to prevent an incident or to deal with an ongoing incident, the competent authority or CSIRT may inform the public of the incident.

---

14   NISD, Annex II and Article 5
15   NISD, Article 14

Obligations to be imposed on digital service providers

A slightly different set of obligations apply to digital service providers, which are defined to include online marketplaces, online search engines and cloud computing services.[1]

Member States are required to ensure that digital service providers:

- manage risk – largely mirroring the equivalent obligation on operators of essential services but with some additional specific details about what elements the measures taken should take into account, including (a) the security of systems and facilities; (b) incident handling; (c) business continuity management; (d) monitoring, auditing and testing; and (e) compliance with international standards;
- minimise the impact of incidents; and
- notify, "*without undue delay*" the competent authority or CSIRT of any incident having a substantial impact on the provision of a digital service they offer within the Union. The public may also be informed of incidents where necessary to prevent or deal with an ongoing incident or where otherwise in the public interest.

To harmonise measures across the Union, the Commission has the power to adopt implementing acts (by 9 August 2017) to clarify what security measures should be adopted and when notification of incidents will be required.

Penalties

Member States are required to set their own penalties for breach of the new NISD requirements. The penalties

---

1   NISD, Annex III

implemented must be effective, proportionate and dissuasive and Member States are required to notify the Commission of the details of these penalties by 9 May 2018.[2]

NEW DOMESTIC CYBER LAWS IN EUROPE

At a Member State level, there have been a raft of initiatives and new laws, such as:

- the UK's "Cyber Essentials" scheme introduced in 2014[3] and the more recent announcement of the creation of a National Cyber Security Centre[4];
- the adoption of a new IT Security Act in Germany in July 2015[5]; and
- the adoption of a new Dutch law in January 2016 on the notification of data leaks, which introduces fines of up to 10% of annual revenues for failing to comply.

Cyber standards

Standards bodies have been busy too, building on existing standards such as ISO27001 and the Payment Card Industry Data Security Standard (PCI-DSS). For example, ISO27017 is a new standard for information security controls for cloud services based on ISO27002.[6] Although not law as

---

2   NISD, Article 21.

3   *See https://www.gov.uk/government/publications/cyber-essentials-scheme-overview*

4   *See https://www.gov.uk/government/publications/national-cyber-security-centre-prospectus*

5   The German IT Security Act - BT-Drs. 18/4096, as amended by the committee on internal affairs BT-Drs. 18/5121

6   *See http://www.iso27001security.com/html/27017.html*

such, these and similar standards are often referred to in guidance issued by regulators and inform the legal standard of care for information security, including what amounts to "appropriate" measures.

THE IMPACT OF BREXIT ON UK CYBER LAWS

On 23 June, the UK voted in a national referendum to leave the European Union. The result has created a great deal of uncertainty, including with respect to the UK's data protection laws.

Some things remain clear:

- the UK's data protection laws will continue to apply, until they are repealed by the UK Parliament;
- if the UK is still in the EU on 25 May 2018, GDPR will come into force automatically;
- "soft" law including security standards such as ISO27001 and PCI-DSS will continue to apply; and
- multinationals established in the UK and in other EU Member States will have to deal with GDPR whatever happens in the UK.

It is likely (though not certain) that the UK will implement NISD by 10 May 2018 as whatever happens during the exit negotiations, the risk of cyber attacks and the damage they could cause to essential services and digital services is still present and a coordinated approach to security standards, incident response and information sharing would seem to be in both the EU's and the UK's best interests.

What is less clear is what happens to the UK's data protection laws if the UK leaves the European Union before May 2018 and what happens to European Union Regulations which are already in force, if the UK leaves after that date.

Various alternatives have been mooted. However it is likely (though again not certain) that the UK will implement laws which largely mirror the requirements of GDPR:

Firstly, because the UK – as a third country – will need to demonstrate an adequate level of protection of personal data to continue to receive personal data from the EU. Although there are other options available, the quickest and most robust way to do this would be to adopt laws equivalent to GDPR and seek a formal adequacy decision from the Commission.

Secondly, because there is broad support for reform of the UK's data protection laws, including calls for much tougher sanctions from key stakeholders such as both Houses of Parliament and the UK's data protection regulator, the Information Commissioner.

Thirdly, because civil servants in Whitehall now have a very long list of laws and treaties to review and renegotiate and will therefore be looking for quick fixes to reduce their workload. As the UK is already on track to implement GDPR it would be relatively simple to continue on that journey albeit some amendments will be required to reflect the fact that the UK will soon be outside of the EU rather than a Member State within it.

CONCLUSIONS

A combination of factors, including the vital importance of secure, trusted information systems to the growth of the digital economy and the increased frequency and seriousness of cyber attacks, has led to the adoption of several significant new laws relevant to cyber security both at an EU wide level and domestically within Member States.

Although well intended, many of these laws are vague, setting general requirements to maintain "appropriate" security without specifying what specific security is required. Similarly, the triggers for notification of cyber breach are not defined to a level of detail that can be easily implemented at an operational level. Guidance is needed from the Commission, from Member State regulators and from the courts as litigation arising from serious cyber incidents will over time inform the legal standard of care, both for security and for notification.

However, organisations cannot wait for this guidance. GDPR, with its revenue based fines, will apply across the EU from May 2018 and most probably laws very similar to GDPR and NISD will apply in the UK too. There is a great deal of work to carry out to prepare for GDPR and NISD to ensure that security systems, incident response procedures and incident response teams are prepared to meet the very demanding new requirements.

PART THREE

Preparation

3.1

HOW MUCH WILL IT COST YOU?

Steve Snaith, RSM Risk Assurance Services

Cyber risk is an escalating threat and one of the most challenging issues facing the world today. Attacks are becoming more frequent, more intense and more sophisticated. Motivations are wide-ranging – from financial gain to threatening critical infrastructure and damage to organisational reputation – and the nature of attacks is constantly changing.

With cyber risk, there is an active adversary so defences need to be increasingly sophisticated to keep pace. A key issue is the source of your cyber risks, which are wide ranging and often sourced from unexpected areas, for example in relation to your:

- Systems
- People
- Business activity
- Customers
- Suppliers
- Image and reputation
- Information about your organisation on the web

These issues collectively constitute a "cyber footprint" that is very often the first stage of any cyber attack. Consequently, for organisations and stakeholders to be better positioned to make appropriate investment decisions regarding risk mitigation, it is important to be able to quantify cyber risk.

In this regard, what would be the value of this risk? There are many examples of quoted financial loss values relating to cyber attacks. Our view is that many of these values are inaccurate, at times overstated and not fundamentally based on sound cost estimation models. At the same time, consider valuing your cyber risk based on a sound basis as a useful exercise to inform your corporate governance framework and cyber control environment, and facilitate methods to improve your controls and the intrinsic value of your cyber control environment.

CYBER RISK EXPOSURE METRIC

Traditional cyber security tends to emphasise the type of attacker, the methods of attack and corresponding control requirements. However, to fully evaluate business risk, RSM considers the characteristics of your business and operating environment, from a risk perspective, as a first stage to inform the type of controls that you need.

Cyber risks differ between various types of organisations, based on a wide variety of risk criteria. The assessment of risk, from both a scope and impact perspective, is of vital importance before any assessment of cyber controls can be carried out as illustrated in Figure 3.1.1.

Figure 3.1.1   Key Components for Assessing the Level of Cyber Risk

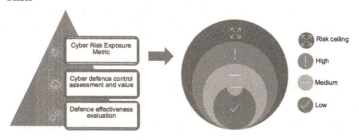

QUANTIFYING YOUR CYBER RISK

From a cyber risk perspective, our methodology begins with the characteristics of your business and operating environment. In this perspective, the cyber risk exposure assessment is designed to identify an organisation's inherent cyber risk before implementing controls, the key components of which we summarise in Figure 3.1.2 below.

Figure 3.1.2   Characteristics Identifying Inherent Cyber Risk

A range of variables are considered in order to determine the risk that you face, including your business environment, the linkages with your stakeholders, the type and number of IT systems that you operate and the on-line 'visibility' of your organisation.

REPORTING YOUR CYBER RISK

Each item of assessment has an associated score which collectively computes your overall risk exposure metric, which is then classified to provide a specific risk conclusion as in Figure 3.1.3.

Figure 3.1.3 Classification of Overall Risk Exposure

These risk metrics helps then to inform the scope, type and nature of cyber controls that you need.

VALUING YOUR CYBER RISK

There are many examples of quoted financial loss values relating to cyber attacks. Our view is that many of these values are inaccurate, at times overstated and not fundamentally based on sound cost estimation models. At the same time, we consider valuing your cyber risk to be a useful exercise to inform your corporate governance framework and cyber control environment.

Having determined your cyber risk exposure level, an organisation can calculate a value for that risk. This is based on criteria which take account of a range of quantitative and qualitative factors, principally:

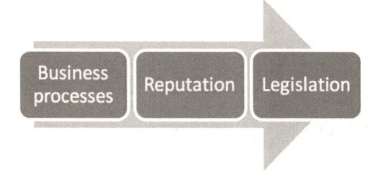

Each key area has an intrinsic value that can be assigned to your organisation, based on the following:

- Assessment of individual business processes, the value of these processes, the percentage of turnover and the risk of each (based on transaction value and volume); and
- Cyber loss business impact assessment for each business process/unit, based on a range of factors including:
  - Value of lost transactions; and
  - Business demand impact through reputational loss.
- The cost of legislation – the level of legislative penalty following loss from a cyber incident.

Following this type of analysis, one method is to produce a matrix analysis of your risks points and associated impact costs in order to produce an indicative cyber risk value as illustrated in Figure 3.1.4.

Figure 3.1.4   Matrix Indictor of Cyber Risk Value

	DAILY TRANSACTIONS VALUE £	ONE OFF INCIDENT COST	CONFIDENTIAL DATA – INCIDENT COST	REPUTATION RELIANCE – RECURRING COST	BUSINESS OPERATING ENVIRONMENT	
Business Process A	350,000		Yes	High		
Business Process B	0		No	Moderate		Controls Effort
Business Process C	725,000		Yes	Low		

Having determined your cyber risk valuation, the next stage is to assess your current control framework, both in terms of design and application. Conclusions on the scope and strength of these controls are then provided. In addition, based on this assessment, the intrinsic value of these controls is assessed and a value indicator determined in relation to your cyber risk.

Opportunities are then identified and evaluated to improve your control environment by strengthening your controls, thereby adding further value to your control framework. Figure 3.1.5 below provides an overview of this approach and the following sections sets out further information regarding our cyber controls maturity assessment methodology.

Figure 3.1.5   Adding Value to the Control Framework

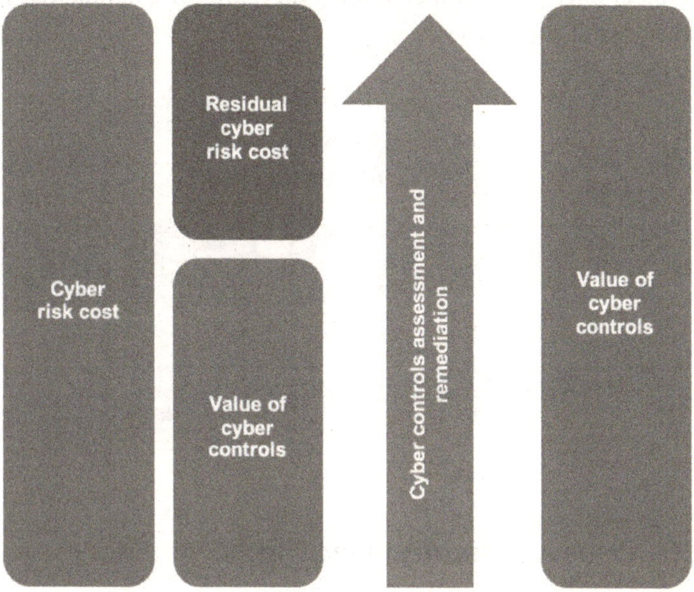

CYBER DEFENCE CONTROL SCORE

An organisations cyber defence scope will be dependent on the strength of its cyber controls. Following the cyber risk exposure assessment, the next stage is to identify and evaluate your cyber defence control framework, its relative level of maturity and its value. This is based on the understanding of your organisation we will have gained from the risk assessment, which is important to ensure our expectations of controls are fully aligned with your business.

METHODOLOGY

The overall controls assessment is based on consideration of the existence, design adequacy and compliance with cyber controls. In this regard, the approach very much follows a typical internal audit methodology. Figure 3.1.6 summarises the overall approach.

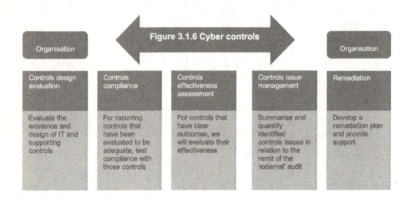

Figure 3.1.6 Cyber controls

Organisation				Organisation
Controls design evaluation	Controls compliance	Controls effectiveness assessment	Controls issue management	Remediation
Evaluate the existence and design of IT and supporting controls	For recurring controls that have been evaluated to be adequate, test compliance with those controls	For controls that have clear outcomes, we will evaluate their effectiveness	Summarise and quantify identified controls issues in relation to the remit of the 'external' audit	Develop a remediation plan and provide support

KEY CONTROL ASSESSMENT COMPONENTS

In terms of evaluating the design and compliance of your cyber control environment, our approach is underpinned by consideration of your policies, processes, governance, education and technical security controls, linked to the key components of people, process and technology within your firm, as set out in Figure 3.1.7.

Figure 3.1.7 Considerations in Evaluating the Design and Compliance of a Cyber Risk Environment

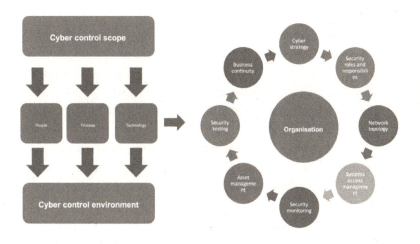

The controls assessment approach is underpinned by 20 specific control areas that form the basis of the assurance methodology, which we summarise in Annex 1 that follows.

ANNEX 1

CYBER CONTROL MATURITY ASSESSMENT

Of key importance regarding a cyber review approach is the provision of cyber controls assessment together with benchmarking against relevant best practice models. In this regard, it is important to underpin a cyber review with a number of standards, in particular GCHG, COBIT and also the IT infrastructure standards set out by such organisations as the SANS Institute. These standards in particular are important in delivering to your requirements, covering high level governance standards and more detailed technical good practice.

Once the control design and application assessment is complete, an organisation can produce a controls maturity analysis based on such a defined process.

MONETISING YOUR CYBER CONTROLS

Following the controls assessment, any opportunities for improvement are quantified and supporting recommendations made. Each control area ultimately correlates back to a component of the initial risk assessment.

The next stage of the controls assessment is to carry out analysis on the valuation of your current cyber control framework. This is correlated to your cyber risk value and the scope, level, alignment and adequacy of your control environment. Once a valuation is determined, opportunities are then assessed to increase the 'value' of your controls through remediation actions identified as part of the controls assessment.

DELIVERABLES

The output of this controls assessment is a formal report that sets out your overall risk metrics and value assessment, controls evaluation.

INCREASING THE VALUE OF YOUR CYBER CONTROLS

There are a wide range of opportunities to increase the value of your controls, all based on primary components that constitute your cyber risk, as illustrated in Figure 3.1.8.

Figure 3.1.8   Opportunities for Increasing the Value of Controls

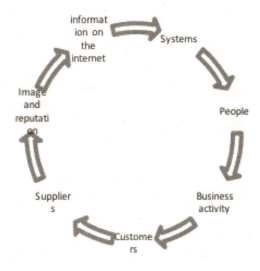

CYBER DEFENCE EFFECTIVENESS EVALUATION

Once the design and compliance of controls is determined, aspects of your cyber control framework can be assessed to form a viewpoint on whether they are actually effective in practice and meet their intended purpose. This is the final phase of a cyber assessment approach:

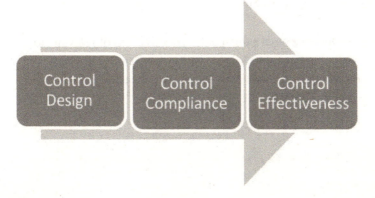

There are a number of areas where we test the effectiveness of your controls. Some example of which are set out below:

- review of Firewall and Intrusion Detection Logs to ascertain traffic restriction controls;
- email spoofing, where on a controlled and agreed basis, we will "spoof" and email to make it appear as a valid Hills Waste Solutions account and send to a sample of staff. The email will be structured to some extent not legitimate regarding the purpose of the email, as we then sample how many staff responded to that email. We have found this to be an excellent technique to test the effectiveness of cyber risk staff awareness controls; and
- systems and vulnerability scanning. As part of our controls maturity assessment, we carry out some automated systems scanning to assess controls design and compliance. By using the same techniques, we also carry out some specific scanning and network probing analysis that is deliberately 'noisy'. Essentially, IDS systems are designed to detect potential unauthorised systems activity. This technique is used to validate if your IDS systems do detect out scanning activity and provides a useful basis to determine the effectiveness of your IDS systems.

Once we have assessed the effectiveness of relevant areas of your cyber control framework, we will provide a viewpoint on whether methods exist to improve the actual effectiveness of your controls.

3.2

A FRAMEWORK FOR CYBER SECURITY

Steve Culp and Chris Thompson,
Accenture Finance & Risk Practice for Financial Services

By taking an integrated view of operational risk and cyber security, financial institutions (FIs) will be better able to protect, monitor and mitigate a wider array of threats. Accenture and Chartis have identified four key building blocks for delivering alignment:

1. *Governance and ownership:* Tangible improvements can be performed by establishing clear lines of responsibility from board level downwards, including organisational definitions where cyber security and operational risk are aligned as part of a formal governance, risk and compliance (GRC) strategy.
2. *Taxonomies and methods:* Bridging the gap between the chief information security office (CISO)/technology or information officer and the chief risk officer (CRO) by creating a common language.
3. *Skills and capabilities:* Multi-disciplinary capabilities and competencies across operational risk and cyber-security should be encouraged. Practitioners should meet

their counterparts in different departments to develop a unified response.

4. *Technology and data:* Technology is a key facilitator for aligning operational and cyber risk strategy. Advanced data management, analytics, modelling and reporting solutions deliver a better response if attacked.

GOVERNANCE AND OWNERSHIP

Top-down governance processes and board-level involvement are important. First and foremost, FIs should establish cyber security processes as mapped across the three lines of risk defence, covering inputs; monitoring of the strategy; and auditing of the strategy (Figure 3.2.1).

Figure 3.2.1   Framework for Aligning Operational Risk with Cyber security

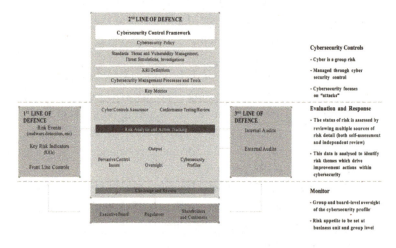

Source: Chartis Research, based on analysis of the risk strategies of several global financial institutions, December 2015

Disaster recovery and business continuity planning (BCP) processes should also be clearly defined and link into an institution's combined operational and cyber risk strategy.

As an example, cyber risk threats and/or vulnerable events, such as wire transfers, should be examined and modelled start-to-finish as part of any FI's procedure, with a "kill chain" clearly established to mitigate risk. Potential points of compromise, responsibilities, and remediation measures should all be detailed at each stage to establish a comprehensive framework.

SKILLS AND CAPABILITIES

Even if cyber security is firmly established as part of the three lines of defence and aligned with operational risk, there is a pronounced industry-wide gap in the skills and training of the professionals tasked with delivering the integrated strategy.

Front line troops with job titles such as CISO or chief technology or information officer (CTO/CIO) tend to have a strong understanding of IT, but in many cases they have limited formal risk management understanding. Similarly, risk managers have a strong understanding of the business and risk concepts needed for a good cyber security response in the event of an attack, but a relatively weak understanding of the complex IT issues involved.

Increasing IT and risk knowledge transfer is critical when aligning cyber security and operational risk. Staff rotation and shadowing may be helpful in promoting mutual comprehension and understanding. Joint competency centers should also be considered, alongside recruitment and incentive strategies to encourage collaboration. Formal knowledge transfer initiatives should have senior management oversight and support. Speed will be of the essence if an FI comes under attack so lines of communication between risk and IT professionals should be open. Regular test scenarios can help.

On-going training is also advisable so that FIs can keep pace with any technological and regulatory changes. Training remains particularly crucial as the vast majority of cyber security incidents start from avoidable human error, such as an employee clicking on a phishing email. While many firms focus on technology and prevention, training and awareness of potential cyber risks from the bottom up is essential.

This should include mandatory awareness of good security practices, and periodic testing of employee responses to potential attacks. In addition, while it is important that training is part of the front office, it is also vitally important that responsibility for basic cyber security does not die out in middle management. In interviews conducted by Chartis and Accenture with firms who had implemented phishing testing, they said that management (including the C-suite) were more likely to respond to phishing emails than front-office employees.

Some may work under the illusion that their firm's security systems are protecting and insulating them, but with respect to cyber security, all employees are potentially on the front line.

TAXONOMIES AND METHODS

If the gap between technological and risk-based knowledge is to be bridged, then the cyber security and operational risk functions need a common language. This can be established by agreeing to a common definition, using International Organization for Standards (ISO) and National Institute of Standards and Technology (NIST) frameworks if desired, and then formulating a responsibility flowchart.

Cyber security risks can be considered to be part of both the operational risk responsibilities and the typical responsibilities of a CTO/CIO/CISO (Figure 3.2.2). Risk and technology re-sponsibilities meet in the middle during cyber security events.

Figure 3.2.2   Risk and Technology Responsibilities

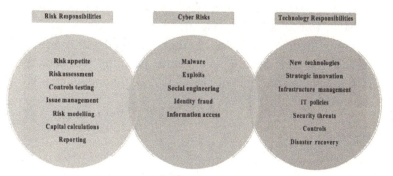

Source: Chartis Research, December 2015

IN SUMMARY – TECHNOLOGY AND DATA ESSENTIALS

Technology and data, whether online or stored on internal systems, are a source of risk but can also be a part of the solution. Good data management, monitoring and analytics can help feed effective processes, communication and early warning mechanisms into the three lines of defence shown in Figure 3.2.1. Technology can help deliver an integrated approach to cyber security and operational risk. A common analytical layer is highly desirable. In addition to the required security tools, Accenture and Chartis consider the following to be important technology elements in any risk-based approach.

Integrated Data Management

FIs may find it hard to attain a holistic view of their operational risks across the whole enterprise because they have many disparate IT systems in use. An effective operational risk management (ORM) system should access risk data from various ORM and cyber security applications, as well as operational sources such as anti-money laundering (AML), third-party risk, and fraud management systems, bringing together KRIs based around internal and external losses, malware detection, standards, patching, and model risk management. Unified risk data models and standards are critical.

Metadata

A metadata-driven approach is essential for this integrated cyber ORM approach to work. Metadata is a means of creating a logical and manageable view of all the risk information available to an organization. Use the latest approaches to enterprise data management (EDM) for a more agile and responsive data environment, enabling auditability, traceability of changes, drill-down workflow and enterprise case management.

Real-Time Reporting

The move towards dynamic and responsive risk management and governance has increased the demand for real-time reporting and the escalation of risk information. The traditional audit-based snapshot approach to ORM should be replaced by dynamic and real-time ORM alerts, including cyber KRIs, in a reformed structure that is supported by automated data feeds. Early warning systems can be created in this manner.

ANOMALY DETECTION

Current anomaly detection systems are often based on searching for known patterns. However, fraud and cyber security analysts require dynamic abilities to look for unpredictable new patterns of attack and relationships. Advanced anomaly detection software goes beyond business rules to include analytics, using advanced methods such as mathematical correlations, predictive modelling and artificial intelligence to acquire a holistic view of entity activity.

INTEGRATED CASE MANAGEMENT

In most FIs, separate business lines use standalone case management databases and workflow solutions for logging and managing alerts. Reporting is also typically done on a siloed basis. Instead, FIs are encouraged to pool information. Pooling cross-organisational, cross-border data is perhaps the most important step down the integration path an FI can take. Unusual patterns of behaviour and new threats can all be identified more quickly with enterprise-wide search capabilities and remediation action can more easily be activated.

3.3

A MAP FOR RESILIENCE

Sam Millar and Helen Vickers
DLA Piper UK

Cyber crime presents an immediate and ever-evolving threat to businesses and individuals across the globe. It is unlikely that this threat will diminish and so businesses must arm themselves with the necessary tools to establish a strong security framework which will effectively mitigate the risk which cyber attacks pose. This chapter explores measures which businesses can take to ensure that their security framework is sufficiently strong to minimise the risk of a cyber attack. Whilst none of these measures is a "quick fix" solution to prevent cyber attacks, when combined and tailored to particular businesses, they will ensure that businesses are well prepared for them.[1]

---

1   This chapter refers to the survey by HM Government and Ipsos MORI, *2016 Cyber Security Breaches Survey 2016*, May 2016 to give an indication of best practice and the extent to which these recommendations are currently being implemented in the market.

IDENTIFY KEY RISKS

The first step a business should take in its implementation of a cyber security strategy is to establish where its key risk areas lie. Businesses should ask themselves where they are most vulnerable to a cyber attack; for example, if they hold or deal with Critical National Infrastructure or if they hold large amounts of sensitive personal data. Establishing where the potential weaknesses lie will allow a business to establish a bespoke framework – the most effective kind of framework.

ACCOUNTABILITY

A recent survey undertaken for the Government established that 34% of businesses employ staff members whose job role specifically includes information security or governance. This is more prevalent amongst medium firms and large firms, especially in the financial or insurance sectors.[2] Smaller organisations, on the other hand, tended to leave cyber security matters to be dealt with by either the IT department or standalone IT enthusiasts.

It is important that responsibility for cyber security is clearly defined and shared with employees. This clarity will assist in raising awareness across the business, as employees will know who to turn to if they have queries or notice anything unusual. Furthermore, if those responsible for cyber security are fully committed to the issue, engagement within the business will happen more naturally than if it is assigned by default to the IT department.

All businesses should ensure that there is an individual (or a team of individuals) who is/are accountable for managing

2   HM Government and Ipsos MORI, *2016 Cyber Security Breaches Survey 2016*, May 2016, p. 23

cyber security risk. Preferably, this would be a senior employee so as to ensure maximum engagement with cyber security across the business. Alternatively, businesses could appoint someone senior to be accountable for managing cyber security risk, whilst also appointing a cyber security "champion" to directly engage on issues within the workforce. This means that ownership of the risk would remain at a senior level but the day-to-day interactions with employees with regards to cyber issues would take place elsewhere. This is particularly important to note if the management of cyber security has been outsourced – the risk should not be transferred to a third party. Best practice suggests there should be an individual within each business responsible for cyber security.

PROCEDURES AND POLICIES

Businesses should establish a comprehensive set of policies and procedures relating to cyber security. Having such policies in place allows for the creation of a security framework. It means that employees are able to refer back to the policies and the business is able to implement training on the cyber security policies. This in turn will create a culture of awareness around cyber security risk.

A recent survey established that relatively few businesses have a formal policy or policies covering cyber security risk. Where such policies are in place, they commonly cover how staff can use the business's IT devices; however, often overlooked are external factors such as the use of removable storage devices or remote working.[3]

Policies and procedures, as a starting point, should cover IT security (including password security), physical security

---

3   HM Government and Ipsos MORI, *2016 Cyber Security Breaches Survey 2016*, May 2016, p. 25

(including the use of storage devices), third party contractors, remote working, background checks and third party contractors. This is by no means an exhaustive list and each business will have to consider which policies are necessary for its business once it has undertaken a risk assessment.

Rather than merely setting out the policy, businesses should explain *why* it has been put in place and which risks it seeks to mitigate – this will foster greater engagement with the policy from within the business. Organisations should also remind employees of the policies which are in place and what they cover – this will help to establish a security culture.[4] Policies should be easily accessible, simply worded and avoid jargon or terminology which may be confusing to employees or which is specific only to one part of a business. These should be easy to navigate with topics clearly identified. It may also be helpful to produce summaries of the key points of the policies if the policies as drafted are particularly lengthy.

Policies should be regularly reviewed to establish whether they need updating. If a policy is updated and significant changes are made to it, businesses should consider notifying employees of this by providing training on the new policy.

Businesses should also consider taking out cyber insurance as a tool to mitigate cyber risk. Policy wording should be carefully reviewed to understand the coverage which the insurance provides. Some insurance policies will go so far as to assist with incident management.

Merely having policies and procedures in place is not sufficient if the policies and procedures are not implemented in practice. When drafting policies, businesses should consider how they will monitor compliance with these policies. Policies

---

4   IS Decisions, *The Insider Threat Security Manifesto: Detecting the Threat from Within*, pp. 24-26

should filter through the entire business rather than risk being stuck in silos of one particular business area. Drafting policies and procedures is the first step – ensuring awareness, regular reviews and compliance will contribute to the creation of a strong security culture.

TRAINING

Training is an essential part of a resilient cyber security framework. Training staff on the potential cyber security threats facing a business as well as training them on the specific policies and procedures in place to combat these threats will educate employees and allow them to engage with the risks. Education of employees means that they will be less of a threat – if the minimum level of awareness amongst employees is raised, the system will be less vulnerable. For example, training may mean that an employee is able to identify a phishing email and therefore will be less likely to open it.

The same 2016 survey discovered that just under a fifth of businesses surveyed had had their staff attend a form of cyber security training in the last 12 months. Training was most common for those in the finance, insurance, administration, IT, real estate and utilities sectors.[5] The most common topics covered in training included: (i) general awareness of cyber security, (ii) culture/attitudes around cyber security, (iii) use of email, web browsers and social networks, (iv) fraudulent attempts to extract important information, (v) what to do if you spot a cyber attack, (vi) use of personally owned devices for business activities, (vii) the impact or cost of cyber security and (viii) remote or

---

5   HM Government and Ipsos MORI, *2016 Cyber Security Breaches Survey 2016*, May 2016, p. 23

mobile working.[6] These chosen topics indicate that training focuses both on raising awareness of cyber security risks as a whole, whilst also focusing on policies around more specific topics such as email working.

Businesses should consider a tailored approach to training, depending on an employee's role within an organisation. For example, introducing separate training for managers which includes guidelines on how to spot unusual behaviour amongst employees. Businesses should ensure that tailored training nevertheless follows a consistent approach. Induction training is particularly important for new joiners to the business. This should point out where the relevant policies and procedures are found on the internal network. However, it is key that this training is repeated periodically to refresh employees' memories as well as to update them if policies have been reviewed and amended.

PHYSICAL AND SYSTEM SECURITY

Physical security and system security are interlinked in the process of building strong defences against cyber attacks. Physical security – protecting the physical areas in the workplace which give access to IT systems – should go hand in hand with system security i.e. protecting the IT systems. Strong physical and system security will create a robust cyber security framework.

When designing a physical security system, the first step businesses should take is to consider which employees need access to critical areas. Access to business assets should be restricted only to those who really need it. Businesses should ask themselves: for whom is access essential? The

---

6   HM Government and Ipsos MORI, *2016 Cyber Security Breaches Survey 2016*, May 2016, p. 24

fewer people with access to critical areas, the smaller the risk becomes.

Access to secured areas should be contingent on receiving a briefing and signing a statement that the person entering the secured area has received that briefing and understands it. Procedures should be put in place for working in secure areas. These should include the use or restrictions on use of removable storage devices and the necessary levels of encryption required for such devices. It may be worth putting a restriction in place to the effect that no employee can be alone in a secured area – two or more people must be present at the same time. A strong CCTV system which is monitored and has footage which is stored in a back-up facility may also be essential.

There are two elements to system security: firstly, overarching measures implemented by the business and secondly, training employees to comply with those measures. IT system security involves the business implementing policies to educate and encourage employees to (*inter alia*) set strong passwords, understand how to handle sensitive data, use mobile devices securely at work and remote work securely. The business should also implement overarching system security, for example, solid and up to date anti-virus software, malware protection and firewalls.

AUDIT

Best practice suggests that organisations should carry out routine monitoring and audits of their systems. Such routine monitoring will also enable businesses to detect any suspicious activity.[1] It is important for a business to be able

---

1   US Department of Justice, Federal Bureau of Investigation, *The Insider Threat*

to spot any irregularities in their systems, whether these are security breaches or financial irregularities. Without regular monitoring, breaches may go undetected.

Regular, thorough audits are the best way for a business to monitor its systems. Businesses should consider conducting regular audits internally as well as externally. Spot audits and unannounced site visits are another way in which businesses can effectively monitor their systems. In the context of cyber security and potentially disruptive cyber attacks, it is particularly important to audit business continuity plans. Penetration testing is also advised for business continuity plans. As part of the audit process, businesses should also regularly monitor their legal obligations to ensure that any policies and procedures are in line with current legislation.

SECURITY CULTURE

The measures outlined above all come together to form a strong defence against cyber attacks and create a strong security culture. As well as implementing strong systems and controls, a business should ensure that the environment it creates is consistent with these measures. Raising awareness of potentially unusual behaviour is important but it must be coupled with a sense that employees are able to report such behaviour without feeling as though they are "snitching" on their colleagues. Cyber security should be a priority and reporting breaches or unusual behaviour should be easy and confidential. Managers must be trained to deal with reports of such behaviour. Businesses may consider setting up a confidential hotline which employees can use to report anything untoward. Businesses may go to great lengths to introduce policies, procedures etc. but if employees are not fully engaged and immersed in the security culture then the framework will not be as effective.

TACKLING INSIDER THREAT

A composite cyber security strategy should not only consider external threats, but also the insider threat. Some of the measures set out above will assist with tackling the insider threat – restricting access to essential business assets to those who need it, establishing a strong security culture as well as ensuring that employees are not left alone in restricted areas.

Pre-employment screening is one method by which insider threat can be mitigated. As well as introducing pre-employment screening for employees, businesses should also ensure that third-party contractors and suppliers meet the requisite pre-employment screening standards. It is advisable to have a policy which sets out the requisite level of background checks to be undertaken on third-party contractors. Businesses could request a warranty of compliance from the organisation providing the contractor. Alternatively, controls could be placed in the contract to ensure that contractors meet the minimum standard required in terms of background checks. Background checks should be repeated, both for employees and for third-party contractors, at various stages during their employment/engagement, rather than just at the outset.

However, it is important to remember that background checking is not a catch-all and should not be relied on as such. A background check may pick up on any criminal history; however, issues such as lifestyle vulnerabilities which may make them more prone to committing cyber attacks (e.g. gambling addiction) will not be covered by the background check. A strong security culture where employees feel comfortable speaking to each other or their line managers is a key defence. Employers should also consider the suitability of that particular candidate to a role – if someone is placed in an unsuitable role it may make them more likely to act out.[2] Background screening should be coupled with the other measures set out above to create a strong defence against cyber attacks, both internally and externally.

BOARD ENGAGEMENT

Board-level engagement is crucial to the development of a strong cyber security defence system. Having cyber security expertise amongst board members can assist others within the business to raise cyber security issues. A recent survey established that a lack of board-level knowledge or understanding was one of the main barriers to firm-wide engagement with cyber security.[3]

Businesses should consider ensuring that the board are given regular updates on cyber security measures. This may involve the cyber security 'champion' updating the board or ensuring that cyber security is an item on the agenda of each board meeting.

CONCLUSION

The establishment of a strong cyber security framework is a process which will take time for businesses to implement. The recommendations referred to above will not by themselves create strong defences against cyber attacks: they must all be combined to create a security system which is reviewed and regularly updated to match the evolving nature of cyber-threats.

---

2   CPNI, *Insider Data Collection Study*, April 2013, p. 14

3   HM Government and Ipsos MORI, *2016 Cyber Security Breaches Survey 2016*, May 2016, p. 16

3.4

PROTECTING FINANCIAL DATA FROM INSIDERS

Cyber IQ and Patrik Heuri

When it comes to information security in the financial services, the insider threat has become something of a bogeyman. It is not simply a case of rooting out those with a lax approach to security or basic cyber hygiene; a greater awareness of the value of data means those who have access to it can be more tempted to steal or sabotage information if they become disgruntled or seek to profit illegally. Know-ing whether others in your tent are doing their part to secure critical data is certainly a difficult ask, but is one that organisations are trying to solve on two fronts: better training and better technology.

Cyber IQ sat down with Patrik Heuri, a global head of security risk at a major bank, who confirmed that both negligence and malicious activity are being considered as equal evils.

"Recent data leaks in financial services that have been found to be intentional have created an anxiety over people risks," he says. "So when it came to delivering concrete solutions and litigation, all the issues surrounding negligence and accidental manipulation are now falling under the same treatment of processes. These recent events have clearly been driven by malicious intention, and the attention of senior management; all the budget to counter this problem has come through that channel, for that purpose. However, in developing these improvements, we've been very happy to completely review the negligence side of human behaviour in the same breath."

Until recently, negligence and all accidental incidents were overseen by IT incident management. Now, some organisations are treating both the malicious and the negligent cases under *security* incident management, which involves increased responsiveness to standard IT measures. This makes sense because when an employee neglects a rule and something goes badly wrong, evidence still has to be gathered and the "scene" still has to be secured just as in a criminal circumstance. A common IT incident, on the other hand, may only require a quick fix and may not even be logged.

"We just developed a new framework for this," Heuri says of his own bank. "Covering both sides of the coin in this way is proving a quick win. By being treated within the malicious activity framework, we're seeing some good results, a better resolution timeframe, and less of an impact to day-today operations."

While efforts are being streamlined to counter the problem, the root causes behind the apparent rise in the insider threat appear to be more complex.

"I see two causes for this trend," Heuri says. "One is an increased level of frustration among employees. This is in accordance with a lower level of general treatment that many employees experience from their employers. As a matter of consequence we do see an increase of people trying to steal information.

"The other is in the way we are introducing new monitoring systems. Through greater monitoring, you get more tickets and more alerts, so an artificial statistic emerges in which more incidents are being reported."

In other words, there is some positivity to be found in the statistics, indicating that while disenfranchisement or disloyalty is perhaps more prevalent, technology and procedure is simply making it easier to notice insider problems.

THE NEW ROAD

A debate has been underway in the InfoSec space thanks in large part to previous high-profile failings. Some have been arguing that the conventional approach to tackling the issue has been systems security focused, whereas the evolution of the digital space and the extent to which data now travels beyond office-wide systems (such as on personal devices) demands that the security focus should likewise transit instead to the data itself.

"I do believe that's exactly the model we're beginning to move towards," says Heuri. "We do have that increased risk because of the inevitable link between people and how much data they have access to, but clearly the data itself is – or should be – the main focus now for these institutions. Sometimes organisations have very complex processes or databanks, and it's just as complex to track a clear path of where the asset is when it comes to securing the data.

"If you take the broad view, financial services are now very committed to securing data and it's shown to be one of their top five risks. It's a rise in what we call 'cyber anxiety'. Organisations would like to secure both the information and the assets all as part of an information protection framework."

With that type of integrated setup, an organisation can get a better picture of all its systems, processes and IT technical controls in one place. This allows for more control of data and in an automated fashion, enabling complete alignment when building in new systems or transferring skilled people into new departments.

TRAINING

Today there is an unprecedented level of commitment to information security training. Data protection onsite and off is not all down to immediate operational staff. Upper management and third parties are often in need of access to sensitive information and simply locking up shop is impractical. Therefore, upskilling the entire ecosystem of data handlers is a must.

While employees are made aware of the risks through rules, policies, guidelines, education the initiation has to come from the board. Senior management has to be involved with this domain because the risk to them is now much greater, with more frequent reporting to the regulators to prove they are upholding standards and more serious financial repercussions for failing to meet them.

Heuri adds: "The clients themselves also need to be educated because often they can be the cause – or at least part of the problem – so they need to be trained in a more attentive manner, such as with fliers, classes, informal training courses, and so on. I would say they do appreciate that level of support from their financial institutions.

"It also needs to involve employees' families. Data protection doesn't stop at the traditional company staff level; it extends further into securing home systems and ensuring others around you are aware of the rules and the risks.

"So, really, you have four areas where you need different levels of education as the risk at the information security domain is amazingly universal. It's put us in a completely new playing field in terms of raising awareness."

Although the benefits of training and standards are on their way, training models are not yet mature enough in general to improve prevention and detection of data leaks. Many organisations react to problems on a case-by-case basis and so lessons also tend to be learned only on a case-by-case basis, feedback is difficult to evaluate, and results hard to quantify. Most courses are frequently styled as checklists – "to-dos" and "not-to-dos", which are rarely refined, updated or embedded.

TECHNOLOGY

In terms of technology, financial services – and indeed many other industries – are investing more than ever into new products that seek to weed out the insider threat before it can take effect. As an example, the upswing in employee monitoring software and analytics, designed to read patterns and flag the potential for disruptive behaviour, is no longer a niche tool. That aside, many still see a lack of innovation when it comes to solving this problem in other, less intrusive ways.

"Most banks are using existing systems that were designed to do something else and have simply been adapted for this domain," explains Heuri. "There is a big demand for new solutions but it's difficult to have when the risk surrounds human behaviour rather than machine activity. My current organisation uses a mixture of every product rather than applying a unified product that can fit all our requirements.

"In terms of Data Loss Prevention (DLP), most of the banks have tools that are in some ways an evolution of the tools that they've been using for logging and monitoring of user activity and compliance on the system, but it's still a case of adapting the old world – controlling systems rather than data – in order to try to mitigate human risk."

Hopes of progressing these tools in an integrated fashion may demand continued involvement from all parties involved in the InfoSec arena, including university researchers, law enforcement agencies, and even psychologists. However, the rate at which unified tools can be designed, tested, produced, emplaced and vetted will, for the time being, lack the speed needed to meet the most immediate or sophisticated threats, so an approach that involves plugging in smaller, verified solutions may continue to be the preferred route in the years ahead.

"It's amazingly complex to get these tools right," Heuri says. "They can't be purely IT products. They need to look at human behaviour, analyse habits, interpret data, auto-correlate trends, and so on. I believe we'll still be a bit behind when it comes to getting these tools to predict or prevent problems before many incidents occur, but they will bridge this gap gradually.

"For the past few years, we're always seeing a threat that's more advanced than the solution, so I'm not sure the gap will be closed soon, but I would love to see some dedicated companies that will really work on people and insider risk, just focusing their efforts on something that could possibly be close to the needs we have today.

"Developing something in a silo by a bank or by a law enforcement agency means we are developing thousands of the same ideas and solutions instead of putting that all together and moving faster. We have the same goals so it makes sense that we need to intensively exchange information. We're working in a regulated environment so we know exactly what we can exchange, and clients love to have a completely transparent interaction. There should be a unified approach to think about scenarios – particularly fraud – about what the next threat may be, and to be one step ahead. That's my vision – let's break down the walls."

Disclaimer: The opinions expressed are the personal opinions of the individuals cited and do not necessarily represent those of Cyber IQ or any other organisation.

PART FOUR

Prevention

4.1

TURNING YOUR PEOPLE INTO YOUR MOST EFFECTIVE DEFENCE: A DIFFERENT APPROACH

Nick Wilding, General Manager, Cyber Resilience
AXELOS Global Best Practice

Board meetings will never be the same again! Since the very public cyber attack on TalkTalk in the UK in late October 2015 and following numerous other high profile CEO apologies, business leaders are now realising the real damage that a cyber attack can have on their organisation. Hard-won reputations – both corporate and personal – competitive advantage and market value are all at risk.

THE GAP BETWEEN AWARENESS AND UNDER-STANDING

Chief executives and non-exec directors in organisations of any size and in any sector increasingly regard cyber attack as one of the greatest risks they face. But typically there remains a gap between their awareness and understanding of the risks which hampers their ability to implement an informed cyber resilience strategy that enables rather than hinders the business and digital transformation strategy. The board have to be asking the questions required to really understand how their cyber risks are affecting their mission, customer trust, intellectual property, commercially sensitive information and operational capabilities. The risks of doing nothing are too great. Critically, they need to understand the role all their people must play in protecting what's most important to the organisation.

The impacts of a successful cyber attack can be devastating. It's been said that a week is a long time in politics – today, 24 hours can be a very long time for a board managing a cyber crisis in the fierce glare of international press and media. The questions will keep coming: "Who has been affected by the attack?" "What information has been lost?" "How did the attack happen?" "Where was the information and how were you protecting it?" "When did you know about the attack?" "What steps are you taking to mitigate the risk and minimise the harm felt by your customers?" Simple questions but difficult to answer authoritatively in front of the cameras, especially when one of the main problems for any board dealing with a crisis following an attack is that they simply won't know all the facts. Is this a situation you want to face and are you ready?

No Organisation Is Bullet-Proof

Rarely a week goes by without us watching or reading about another organisation dealing with an embarrassing cyber attack in the media. The harsh reality in today's hyper-connected age is that no organisation can be totally bullet-proof, no organisation can ever say they're safe from attack and no organisation or individual is immune from being targeted. All leadership teams need to understand that they are being attacked, may well already have been compromised and that the risks they face will continue to evolve, adapt and become more persistent. As Ian Livingston, former Chief Executive of the BT Group said at Davos in January 2013:

> "There are two types of CEO, those that know their systems are being hacked – and those that don't. For pretty much any company I've come across, it should be one of the top three risks."

Cyber attacks are now 'business as usual' and cyber resilience should be a standard agenda item at board meetings.

THE LIMITATIONS OF TECHNOLOGY

Global investment in cyber security technologies is continuing to rise. PWC's '*Global State of Information Security Survey 2016*' reports that they "...discovered more than 430 million unique new pieces of malware in 2015, up 36 percent from the year before. Perhaps what is most remarkable is that these numbers no longer surprise us. As real life and online become indistinguishable from each other, cyber crime has become a part of our daily lives. Attacks against businesses and nations hit the headlines with such regularity that we've become numb to the sheer volume and acceleration of cyber threats."

But there's something missing between our continued investment in, and expectation that, technology can solve the problem and the growing number of attacks.

Tom Farley, President of the New York Stock Exchange, said in his introduction to '*Navigating the Digital Age: the definitive cyber security guide for directors and officers*' in 2015:

"It is important companies remain vigilant, taking steps to proactively and intelligently address cyber security risks within their organisation. Beyond the technological solutions developed to defend and combat breaches, we can accomplish even more through better training, awareness and insight on human behaviour. Confidence, after all, is not a measure of technological systems, but of the people who are entrusted to manage them."

THE HUMAN FACTOR

Verizon's 2015 annual data breach report highlighted one stark fact. The great majority – estimated to be 90% – of successful cyber attacks succeed because of human error. Anyone in any organisation, irrespective of their role or seniority, can enable an attack to succeed through their unwitting actions. Cyber-attackers have the upper hand here – they only need to be successful once – whereas all your people have to be aware and capable of making the right decisions, every time they're exposed to different cyber risks. How confident are you that your people are displaying the appropriate behaviours and understand the practical things they need to do to effectively protect the information and systems that are most precious and valuable to you?

The human factor means organisations need to be thinking about cyber *resilience* not just cyber *security*. Cyber resilience can be described as the ability of any organisation to prevent, detect, respond and recover from the impacts of an attack with minimal damage to their reputation and competitive advantage.

The challenge appears clear. All our people must play a more significant and specific role in our organisational resilience. How many times do we read or hear that our staff are our weakest link? Yet they are only as weak as the strength of the awareness learning we provide them. Does it engage? Is it relevant to the learner? Does it provide simple, practical guidance? Is it focused on giving them the confidence to change their existing behaviours and to discuss incidents with their colleagues?

EDUCATION AND TRAINING

The sad truth is that most organisations typically only educate their people in their annual information security awareness e-Learning. It's widely acknowledged that this yearly compliance "tick-box" approach to learning fails to engage and has little or no impact on people's cyber behaviours.

So Can E-Learning Really Change Behaviours?

Yes. But not in its current form – a one-off course, required once, designed once, delivered once, completed once and forgotten at once. The annual one-off course usually takes over an hour to complete and this ignores some simple rules for effective learning. Over 100 years ago Hermann Ebbinghaus, an eminent German psychologist, pioneered the experimental study of memory and is known for identifying the "forgetting curve". He found that 40% of information presented as learning is forgotten in the first 20 minutes, more than half of all information is forgotten after one hour and only a fifth of all information is remembered after one day.

With multiple cyber attacks now routinely targeting and threatening our most sensitive and valuable information, forgetting is no longer an option. Ignorance isn't a defence anymore. The risks and impacts are too great.

In this vital area of staff training and development, one size doesn't fit all. The current "all staff, once a year" approach simply does not influence or change behaviours. At best it reminds us of some essentials, at worst it's treated as unnecessary, a distraction and as "something I have to do...or else". Annual e-Learning will not instil and sustain the cyber resilient behaviours that employees need today. We're trying to 'programme' our people in the same way we programme computers: to do certain things, in defined ways at certain times. This approach doesn't work with people.

LEARNING TECHNIQUES

Instead, there needs to be a range of learning techniques that truly engage all our people, embedding and sustaining the resilient behaviours required to more effectively protect an organisation's most sensitive and valuable information and systems.

What generally dictates the capability and performance of anyone working anywhere is the relevance and effectiveness of the training and learning they're given and the behaviours they adopt as a result of this. During January 2016, AXELOS RESILIA carried out research with IPSOS Mori amongst those responsible for information security awareness learning in their organisations. We wanted to find out how well-prepared the UK's workforce is for a cyber attack in the companies they work for. The results were telling.

While it was positive to note that 99% of business executives responsible for cyber awareness learning said that information security awareness learning was "important to minimise the risk of security breaches", less than a third of them (28%) judged their organisation's cyber security awareness learning as "very effective" at changing staff behaviour. A similar minority (32%) were "very confident" that the learning was relevant to staff, whilst 62% were only "fairly confident" that their learning was relevant.

This comparatively low level of corporate confidence in the ability of people to deal with a potential cyber attack is simply not good enough in an era where cyber crime has become 'business as usual'. It reflects either a lack of understanding, or a state of denial, about the impact that a successful cyber attack can have on a business: reputational damage, loss in competitive advantage and disrupted operations. Organisations cannot continue to accept this level of employee awareness and competence in the face of sophisticated cyber criminals who are constantly adapting their methods to target us. Imagine how your customers would respond if told that "we're fairly confident that your precious information is safe from attack". Equally, reporting to a board of directors that the level of confidence in the organisation's information security awareness is only "fair" would be given short shrift. If company boards are not asking those responsible about the current effectiveness of their awareness learning among their people and what is being done to improve their cyber resilience, then they should be. Now!

We need to understand that we all learn differently and at different speeds. We need to provide the training that instils our people with the confidence to share and discuss experiences, to get involved in the process, to champion resilience and to learn and adapt.

The picture of preparedness painted by our research suggests that the current, compliance-based approach relied upon by the majority of organisations is failing.

A NEW APPROACH

A new approach is required – one where information security or cyber awareness learning is conceived as a continuous and sustainable campaign over time. Just as our technical security controls will evolve and adapt to suit changing cyber threats and vulnerabilities, so we need to ensure all our people maintain their awareness and are provided with the appropriate practical guidance on a continual basis that fits the needs and requirements of the particular organisation.

Here are some simple guiding principles towards ensuring your cyber awareness learning campaign remains effective and engaging:

1. **People pay attention to leaders:** Getting the buy-in and involvement of those at the top can highlight the positive benefits of resilient behaviours, assist in rewarding and inspiring all staff and illustrate just how seriously the leadership team is committed to protecting their organisation's most sensitive information and systems.

2. **Memories are fragile:** Always plan to reinforce, refresh and evolve the learning content and delivery techniques with your staff on a regular basis. Combining engaging online learning content and formats with offline activities such as live events, competitions, surveys and team learning sessions can help sustain and instill the understanding and importance of new behaviours.

3. **People learn differently:** Develop your campaign around a lively mix of different online formats – games, animation, simulations, and videos – to enable people to choose their preferred learning style but which ultimately all provide the same learning outcomes. Exploiting the latest developments in game play for example can assist in immersing the learner in the problem and helps to provide simple, pragmatic advice for how to 'beat' the attack.

4. **People remember stories over facts:** Critically, ensure you fix a message in your learner's minds by appealing to their hearts. Great campaigns have great stories to

tell. The cyberattack statistics are plain to see and yet organisations still remain highly vulnerable to even the simplest attacks. Talk about business impacts and personal consequences, not technology and jargon.

A great example of this is *Whaling for Beginners*, a short story thriller written for RESILIA that follows the journey made by Jim Baines, the CEO of a US packaging company, as he realizes just how catastrophic a cyber attack can be and how easily hard won reputations and competitive advantage can be irreparably damaged.

5. **Use every means at your disposal:** Always stay agile, always adapt, fine tune, pilot new techniques and react quickly to the latest attack stories and how they affect your people. Also consider identifying team "champions" and "mentors" who you can involve in the design, not just in the learning. This has been seen to help build a powerful culture from the bottom-up not just from the top-down.

As phishing attacks and social engineering continue to account for the large majority of successful cyberttacks, influencing and improving human behaviours must sit at the heart of any effective cyber resilience strategy and response. The future success of an organisation will depend on its people recognising their part in the operational health of the organisation and feeling valued in that responsibility.

INFLUENCING AND IMPROVING HUMAN BEHAVIOURS

Effective awareness learning must provide your people with the knowledge, skills and confidence to adopt new behaviours designed to grow your firm's cyber resilience. Use a range of innovative learning tools and techniques, focused on building, maintaining and measuring the effectiveness of the awareness learning provided to the workforce. This approach differs from the traditional, yearly compliance-driven learning in a number of ways:

- It provides ongoing, short, practical advice that minimises day-to-day disruption
- Its adaptive and personalised content can be matched to learner preferences for how they learn
- It offers engaging, competitive and fun content for effective learning
- It provides measurable outcomes for an organisation and their people based on skills and knowledge improvement
- It can meet existing compliance requirements of regulatory bodies as appropriate.

Any awareness learning also needs to be continually developed to ensure the content provided and techniques used to deliver the learning remain up-to-date, relevant and role and sector specific. And while the level and quality of the cyber awareness learning is clearly alarming, so is the misplaced confidence in technology to prevent cyber breaches. Wherever there are people in an organisation – from the executive suite to the shop floor – there are vulnerabilities.

Adopting a new approach to cyber awareness learning across your whole organisation and wider partner/supplier ecosystem will provide greater resilience and tangible business value. By designing, implementing and managing effective and regular awareness learning you will:

- Reduce your risk of a successful and damaging cyber attack
- Grow a cyber-smart and engaged workforce
- Have an effective, efficient and consistent delivery mechanism

- Have an effective cyber control that addresses your people based cyber risk
- Have an effective, consistent and efficient addition to your security controls environment.

In their *'Cyber Risk Oversight for Boards'* the US National Association of Corporate Directors stated in 2015:

> "Cyber resilience is a serious corporate risk issue affecting virtually all levels of significant business activity."

Ultimately, as one director put it: "Cyber security is a human issue."

The senior vice president and chief information security officer of a leading US retail bank also said recently: "Cyber resilience comes down to having an organisation of people who are cyber aware, curious, asking the right questions, actively and continually engaged in learning and who are not just ticking the box."

Without all of this in place it is just a matter of time before you'll be expected to respond to a successful attack or significant data breach. Where would you rather be?

4.2

MAKING YOUR BUSINESS CYBER RESILIENT

Steve Culp, Chris Thompson and Jon Narveson,
Accenture Finance & Risk Practice for Financial Services

Although the rise of digital has revolutionised how businesses work and serve their customers, it has also added new and more severe dimensions of risk, particularly for financial services firms.

Coping with these digital risks is now an urgent matter. Cyber attacks are dramatically increasing. The number of data breaches rose 23 percent in 2014. Five out of every six large companies (those with more than 2,500 employees) were attacked in 2014, a 40 percent increase over the previous year.

Small and medium-sized businesses also saw an increase, with attacks rising 26 percent and 30 percent respectively.[1]

---

1 *Internet Security Threat Report*, Symantec, April 2015, Volume 20. Access at: http://www.symantec.com/connect/blogs/2015-internet-security-threat-report-attackers-are-bigger-bolder-and-faster.

In 2015, a record was set with nine mega-breaches reported (each mega-breach represents more than 10 million records).[2]

THE GROWING RISKS AND COSTS OF CYBER ATTACKS

The costs of cyber attacks are also soaring — measured in loss of revenue, customer trust and loyalty, and costs of litigation and higher insurance premiums. According to a global insurer, cyber attacks cost businesses as much as $400 billion a year, including the initial damage as well as ongoing disruption.[3] By 2020, research firm Gartner expects companies across the globe will spend about $170 billion on cyber security, a growth rate of almost 10 percent over the next four years.[4] BITS, the technology policy division of the Financial Services Roundtable, reports that the demand for cyber security insurance increased by 21 percent across all industries in 2014.[5] Because many incidents go undetected and impacts may not always be immediately visible, the true scale of the problem is most likely even greater.

The frequency and intensity of digital risks, as well as their costs, is now affecting agency oversight. Standard

---

2 *Internet Security Threat Report*, Symantec, April 2016, Volume 21. Access at: https://www.symantec.com/content/dam/symantec/docs/reports/istr-21-2016-en.pdf.

3 *Lloyd's CEO: Cyber attacks cost companies $400 billion every year*, Fortune, January 23, 2015.
Access at: http://fortune.com/2015/01/23/cyber-attack-insurance-lloyds/

4 *Companies Lose $400 Billion to Hackers Each Year*, Inc., September 8, 2015. Access at: http://www.inc.com/will-yakowicz/cyberattacks-cost-companies-400-billion-each-year.html

5 Ibid.

& Poor's Financial Services LLC, a part of McGraw Hill Financial (S&P), announced that it was considering firms' cyber security capabilities in their credit ratings and could downgrade firms where cyber weakness has been identified.[6] We expect others to follow.

In the face of this threat and its associated developments, financial services firms should now think differently about digital risk management. The protective steps they are taking are important but not enough. Cyber attacks are not an "if" but a "when and how." The threats are too frequent and too varied. Attackers are nimble and adapt quickly. They require little capital investment and resources to devise and mount their attacks. Many criminals are already inside a company and breaches are inevitable in our view. Traditional preventative measures can slow them down but not ultimately stop them. Financial services firms cannot protect themselves from cyber attacks 100 per cent of the time. In addition to increasing the sophistication of their barriers, financial institutions also need to increase their resilience – their ability to bounce back from an attack or other security event and resume normal operations.

That means that firms should think differently. In addition to improving their traditional preventative measures, they also should make themselves cyber resilient.

WHAT IS CYBER RESILIENCY?

Cyber resiliency is the ability to operate the business processes in normal and adverse scenarios without adverse outcomes.

---

6   *Banks With Weak Cyber security Could Be Downgraded: S&P*, CFO, September 29, 2015 Access at: http://ww2.cfo.com/ cyber-security-technology/2015/09/banks-weak-cybersecurity-downgraded-sp/

Specifically, resiliency strengthens the firm's ability to identify, prevent, detect and respond to process or technology failures and recover, while reducing customer harm, reputational damage and financial loss.

Resilient businesses have several common characteristics:

* More secure processes and systems;
* Strong controls with a strong control environment;
* A solid risk culture;
* Digitised and automated processes.

To become more cyber resilient, firms need to not only incorporate the front-end security, but also the business risk/reward decision making, risk management and control techniques, as well as secure employee adoption. Only then can they expect to more effectively mitigate the likelihood of an event and reduce the impact if one does occur.

Creating cyber resiliency should span business processes and infrastructure. For example, it should include re-architecting business processes to reduce the access, dissemination, and reliance on highly sensitive data. It should also involve re-architecting infrastructure and systems to limit the extent of potential damage when an attack occurs or systems and processes fail. And it may include re-working ways in which legal and liability protections are incorporated into service agreements to prevent fraud-related losses or expenses associated with remediating impacted customers.

THREE PILLARS OF CYBER RESILIENCE

Some firms may limit cyber resilience and risk management to just an exercise of "being prepared" for a worst-case scenario. Being prepared is certainly an important part of resilience because having a plan can help shape a proper response in a stressed scenario. However, cyber risks are multi-dimensional and cyber resilience should focus on managing three types of risks in particular (see Figure 4.2.1.).

Figure 4.2.1 Summary of Cyber Risks, Consequences and Responses

	IT Systems and Infrastructure Risks	Operational Risks	Fraud and Financial Crime
What are the risks?	• Expansion of digital capabilities increase exposure points for penetration • Data loss, including Personally Identifiable Information (PII), Intellectual Property (IP), and Material Non-Public Information (MNPI) • System failure, loss of system control or complete system takeover	• Brand and reputational risks associated with loss of trust • Failure to operate in a stable or stressed environment leading to financial losses • Loss of intangible value and goodwill • Legal and regulatory risks due to non-compliance	• Internal fraud from employees and third parties • External fraud from criminal activities • Money laundering • Account take-over • Social engineering

What are the consequences?	• Time intensive/high cost to repair • Increased vulnerabilities/ exposure • Loss of trust/ reputational risk • No longer able to control data once extracted from source	• Inability to operate/run the business • Loss events impacting risk capital and profitability • Unknown vulnerabilities due to weak processes or controls	• High velocity and frequency of incidents limit detection and increase costs • Lost revenue and profit • Increased regulatory costs and fines
What are the responses?	• Embrace digital processes and controls for agility and prevention • Re-architect how systems and processes are designed and implemented • Increase scope of accountability beyond technology and into the business	• Regular planning and oversight from a firm-wide perspective with business and technology accountability • Improve the effectiveness of current process and system controls	• A combined business and technology approach • Improved controls in IT risk and operational risk which reduce probability of fraud and financial crime

Source: Accenture, November 2015

IT SYSTEMS AND INFRASTRUCTURE RISKS

Technology systems and infrastructure are often "ground zero" for cyber attacks and other breaches, so technology risk management is increasingly important to a cyber resilient firm. At a minimum, leading technology risk management programmes incorporate the following:

- *Application development standards:* How applications, systems and infrastructure are architected and developed to reduce risk. Techniques may include firewalls, access management, encryption and transmission techniques.
- *Systems and data surveillance:* Monitoring and surveillance techniques for identifying, assessing and responding to potential vulnerabilities or breaches.
- *Penetration testing:* Establishing the resilience of the infrastructure to attacks and proactively identifying where vulnerabilities may occur.

Technology risk management programmes should not exist in a silo or as an independent function. Instead they should be integrated with other risk management programmes such as operational risk and compliance.

Technology risk management also needs greater visibility in the appropriate business governance and management routines. This is important both for funding and investment in mitigating the cyber risk, as well as advising and directing the business as future decisions are made.

OPERATIONAL RISKS

Operational risks refer to the potential for a firm's business processes or technology infrastructure to fail, with adverse consequences such as being unable to communicate with customers, generate transactions or conduct billing. Operational risks also impact brand and reputation, leading to the potential for losses in intangible value as well as actual sales and revenue.

An operational risk management programme should incorporate the following elements as part of building cyber resiliency:

- ***Risk appetite:*** Levels that define and incorporate the tolerance and parameters by which resiliency will be established for cyber risk management programs and how cyber events will be handled.
- ***Process and technology risk assessments:*** Processes that examine gaps in controls around business processes, products or services.
- ***Control reviews:*** Effectiveness assessments that show evidence of proper controls that can prevent or detect cyber risk-related losses.

- ***Integrated framework:*** A cyber risk framework for identifying, preventing, detecting and responding to cyber risks.

A resilient organisation recognises that cyber attacks and cyber risks evolve rapidly, occur with high frequency and are unrelenting — meaning they cannot easily be isolated and managed. Therefore, the risk management models should be nimble, flexible and proactive with regard to how governance, policy, technology and processes are implemented.

Most importantly, the operational risk capability should be at the forefront of quantifying the risk exposure. That means working horizontally between chief risk officer (CRO), chief information officer (CIO) and chief operations officer (COO) to encourage proper investment, maintenance and control across multiple points of entry and attack.

FRAUD AND FINANCIAL CRIME

Fraud and financial crime can result from the exploitation of vulnerabilities in payment systems, digital banking services, electronic trading and failed controls in business processes, technology and even third-party organisations. Furthermore, cyber criminals often rely on the financial institution's infrastructure to perpetrate and carry out their schemes, masking themselves as legitimate customers.

Fraud and financial crime losses can come either from large one-time events or frequent, small and harder-to-detect low-cost events. The fraud costs associated with a firm's customers also impact them because they bear the brunt of losses associated with attacks using stolen identities, credit cards and account remediation — costly services for events not within their direct control.

A resilient organisation should incorporate the following elements in its fraud and financial crime risk management programmes:

- *Surveillance:* The ability to monitor and detect anomalies inside the institution is an important aspect of identifying and controlling losses tied to cyber risk.
- *Detective business processes:* Business processes that are designed to be both compliant and detective of criminal or nefarious activities in a proactive management technique.
- *Industry data sharing:* Even with new regulations on the horizon that allow data sharing of events with the federal government, industry sharing of attack data to improve detection and response techniques can help reduce unexpected losses tied to fraud and financial crime.

4.3

COUNTERMEASURES TO ADVANCED THREATS

Nick Ioannou

Depending on which vendor security report you read, there are x number of million malware variants, growing at a rate of y per second, any of which could pose a serious threat to your business. But as well as dealing with all of these, you also need to be able to protect against targeted advanced threats against you or, to put it simply, the unknown threats. If a criminal organisation targets you and invests some time and money, the odds are heavily stacked in their favour, because as the saying goes, they only need to be lucky once; you need to be lucky every time. In today's world of vulnerabilities in their hundreds on an average corporate computer and the black market trade of exploits, protecting your business is a massive undertaking, for which sometimes not only are the goalposts moving, but the whole playing field can change overnight too.

THE ODDS ARE IN FAVOUR OF THE CRIMINAL

The cost of someone creating targeted malware has plummeted in recent years and so has the technical knowledge required, due to the perfect storm of automation, cloud computing and "crime as a service" offerings. As crazy as it seems, criminals are offering support contracts and help desk features for their cloud services to other criminals. It can now be as simple as a few clicks to create a one off piece of malware, coupled with information gleaned from social media. The odds are in the criminal's favour. You could also be targeted as a stepping stone to get to one of your clients, so the question of "why would anyone target us?" becomes: "has anyone targeted us yet and would we necessarily know if they had?"

Investing in any security solution must be with the understanding that it will not give you 100% protection, no matter what the marketing brochure or sales rep says. Also, the cost of a solution does not always correspond with its level of protection; so just because you are spending a lot, it does not always mean you are spending it wisely. Therefore, my recommendation is to have a layered approach to security, which is in the reach of SMEs if you choose security solutions that scale both up and down, with the same cost per person, whether you are an enterprise or small business.

PLUGGING THE GAPS

The first step though is to take a big step back and look at what you have in place with regards to your security solutions and identify the gaps in your prevention and reporting strategies. Look at the routes and scenarios through which malware can enter your business, which for me is email attachments, internet links, web browsing and USB devices. To address this, I had put in place a wide range of security solutions including anti-malware, patch management, web traffic filtering, DNS filtering, email filtering, email hyperlink real-time filtering and layer 7 UTM firewalls. Yet when it came to advanced targeted threats, I had noticeable gaps in my security. The major gaps for me were too many users who were running their computers with system administrator privileges and I had limited ability to block an unknown application. I would also prefer to open anything from the internet in a protected sandbox environment. So once identified, I set about looking for solutions to plug these gaps.

MANAGING VULNERABILITIES

Mitigating vulnerabilities is a major factor in stopping advanced threats as many will try to use known exploits and patch management, while critical, still leaves hundreds of active vulnerabilities in the majority of systems, but there are solutions. The principle of least privilege when it comes to user admin rights goes a long way into mitigating a large percentage of vulnerabilities. Making everyone login as a standard user also helps stop them from doing things they are not supposed to do, or being tricked into doing them. Technically it can have a zero cost to implement as it is a built in operating system function and recommended best practice; yet thousands of companies do not implement it for a variety of reasons. Historical workarounds for custom software is often cited and the endless administrator prompts to update software or install anything new can cause so much disruption, that administrator rights are often restored.

BALANCING SECURITY WITH PRODUCTIVITY

The balance between productivity and security is a delicate one and as a reduction in productivity can easily be measured, while increased security cannot, it is easy to have good security measures reversed due to reduced productivity. A solution to avoid this is privilege management software, which will intercept any administrator credential requests and either pass on the information automatically or deny the request based on pre-defined rules, removing the need for the user to have to type anything or need to actually know the administrator password. Individual trusted applications can also be elevated to run with administrator credentials, so any old workarounds are still available to the users, but restricted to the applications that require it. It's a bit like giving users just their hotel room key, rather than the master key that opens every room.

BLOCKING UNKNOWN MALWARE

Now the problem we are faced with is how do you block an unknown malware application, something that doesn't yet exist or is created specifically to target your business or industry? Network analysis hardware, while proven, is expensive as it can be required at each of your business premises to be effective and needs constant updating and so it tends to be out of the reach of many SMEs. Assuming that all your users' internet traffic is going through these boxes, which is often not the case in today's mobile world, immediately you have a gap that needs to be addressed. Therefore, one solution is to completely flip the problem on its head and instead of trying to block the unknown, only allow the known and trusted. Instead of working out what to block and trying to maintain the ever growing list (according to some security firms at a rate of 8 per second) the focus is on working out what to allow to run on your computers.

WHITELISTING AND ITS LIMITATIONS

Typically, this is known as application "whitelisting" or application control and while a relatively simple concept, is not easy to implement given the vast number of component applications all created by a wide range of software companies in a typical corporate computer. A typical Windows computer with MS Office is made up of thousands of individual applications, all of which could be changed, replaced or removed by an update patch or new version of the software. The list of what applications are trusted and known rapidly becomes a list of trusted software publishers in order to keep up with pace of change.

The danger though of stopping colleagues from working and being productive after a string of software updates is very real in a badly configured application whitelisting solution. Scenarios like a software company being sold or a merger could have implications for an application whitelisting solution as the next software update normally includes a name or publisher change, which could result in the application being falsely blocked. Depending on your business setup, this could cause a little inconvenience or a lot of upheaval and problems if it was a critical software application.

In order to minimise the risk of falsely blocking trusted applications, just about every application whitelisting solution initially has a listen or investigation mode to work out what programmes your users have in order to establish a baseline. It is important to get this stage right, because once you turn on the blocking of untrusted applications, you could be stopping colleagues from being productive and they could lose faith in the security solution and use their rank to request workarounds or to turn off the solution on their computer in the name of meeting a deadline.

So a pilot scheme is typically recommended, because in most cases there will be snags and issues that will need to be addressed. Often this is due to users running software you were not aware of (the shadow IT problem) or undocumented software that was created or purchased for a small team. For my pilot scheme, I rolled out the solution to everyone in a listen and report only mode as a few individuals like our accounts department had niche software, but then only turned on the application blocking for a few people who were happy to test the solution. Even then things didn't go smoothly, due to a clash of security software caused by our banking software and a few Microsoft Windows 10 issues. Once the issues are resolved, those machines can then be added to the pool to actively block, but expect to have to remove machines if you need to, as issues surface during the pilot scheme.

Application whitelisting solutions can also block things based on where they originated, whether from the internet, the local machine, a network share or USB device. This gives you greater flexibility and granularity when it comes to deciding if an application is trustworthy, so while an application will run from the local machine, it can be set to be blocked if run from the internet or a USB device. Any rules and configurations you make can be updated at any time and as far as I am concerned, expecting a totally "set and forget" environment is unrealistic.

In fact, the whole listen and approval stage is an ongoing process, so monitoring of the system is required as well as reporting on events in order to minimise any false positives and investigate incidences of escalated privileges or run requests of unknown software. If a malicious piece of software makes a run request and is denied, that is all well and good, but now you need to investigate how the user ended up in the situation in the first place. This can help identify holes and flaws in your other security defences, so you can take the necessary steps to address the issues as something must be amiss. It's a bit like having thieves attempt to open a virtually uncrackable vault in a bank; the main concern is not whether they can crack the safe, but how they managed to get into the vault room in the first place.

Choosing Your Security Solution

The security solution I rolled out was a combined privilege management and application whitelisting hosted Software as a Service (SaaS) platform, as I didn't want any additional hardware in the server racks or the VPN links being burdened with additional traffic. There are lots of different solutions and price points to match, but the SaaS requirement limited my choices somewhat, although I expect that to change in the future, if it hasn't already done so.

One word of warning is that some of the solutions come with consultancy fees to configure the system, while others do not; something that needs to be considered when evaluating a solution. If you buy the software/hardware, a 20% maintenance charge seems to be the norm for many of the systems, which was another reason for my SaaS choice. My solution didn't include web sandboxing, but given the price-point and it being both available as a hosted platform or on-premise installation it was a compromise I was willing to make. As every business is different, my choice may not suit your business; even I may be using a different system in 2-3 years' time, if it doesn't do what it is intended to do or a much better alternative becomes available and a move is justified.

BACK TO BASICS

While this chapter is focusing on countermeasures to advanced threats it is important not to forget the basics. Good security is an ongoing process that needs constant attention, with user education factored in as well technological solutions. New technological advances in malware or a bug in an operating system update could make any security solution useless, so it is important to be able to identify suspicious web traffic, especially command and control traffic by malware infections. Some companies offer an incident response service as part of a security solution as well as an individual service offering.

Speed is of the essence when it comes to incident response and if you do not have a 24/7 help desk or security team to monitor potential breaches and security incidents, it may be wise to outsource that function. Having the most sophisticated reporting tools is not much use if there is no one to act upon an incident that occurs at midnight. Nine hours is a long time to cause some serious damage, encrypt or steal data, before anyone is able to respond. Given that an attack could originate from pretty much anywhere in the world, this means that it could occur any time of the day due to the different time zones. In fact, it makes sense to attack countries while most of the people are sleeping, because most of the time there is no one to react. Assuming that there is something to react to; that is, because once an infection from an advanced threat has been successful, it can often lie dormant for weeks or months.

Anyone who has spent time and money creating a one off advanced piece of malware will probably also have put some thought into the later stages. Some of the effects may be nothing more than smoke and mirrors, to distract you from the real goal. For example, the target may be your accounts department or FD, in order to send out emails telling all your customers that your BACS bank details have changed and to pay all future invoices to a new bank account. Meanwhile, various servers are hit with ransomware and databases are copied into a cloud server under their control. You think you are dealing with a ransomware attack and data breach, so could easily miss whatever else the criminals may have also done.

Another scenario is where the real target is getting your server to farm in your data centre to mine for crypto-currencies without you realising. Criminals may be after your processing power or bandwidth rather than your information. They may also be shorting shares in your company; so other than to cause maximum disruption and damage to your company reputation, they are not actually after anything as such within your company. Therefore, after any type of infection, it is worth checking everything, especially any tamper proof logs or email archives, since the criminals cannot erase their tracks in these systems.

You can also set up your own honeypot accounts within your client databases and contact lists, which no one internally ever sends emails to. For the cost of a couple of privately listed domain names, which route emails back to your IT department, this can be an effective way of being alerted to suspicious outgoing emails or the fact that someone has copied your client database.

Protecting your company from advanced threats is no easy task, but the right mix of layered security solutions that includes application control and privileged rights management, as well as all the usual filtering technologies, will go a long way towards protecting you. Just remember to invest in the monitoring of your solutions and expect issues to arise, no matter how amazing the sales rep says it is.

PART FIVE

Protection and Response

5.1

MANAGING INCIDENTS AND INTERNAL SECURITY BREACHES

Julian Cracknell, BAE Systems Applied Intelligence

As cyber hackers become more sophisticated and the volume of attacks escalates, it is almost inevitable that every organisation will at some stage experience a cyber attack or breach. In response to the continual and evolving cyber threat, all organisations need to ensure that their defensive measures are equipped to deal with the threats that they are facing. However, securing end-points and digital perimeters with firewalls, intrusion detection and data loss prevention is no longer enough. It is now just as important to mitigate against the consequences of a breach.

In a recent survey that BAE Systems conducted with large enterprises, over 57 per cent of respondents had experienced a cyber attack in the previous 12 months, with a quarter experiencing a breach in the previous month. Cyber criminals are getting smarter, sharing resources and ideas. They understand what tools are available to prevent their attacks, engineer their tactics accordingly and persevere with long term strategies until they are successful.

The impact of an attack can be devastating; stolen intellectual property can destroy competitive advantage, breached customer data can extinguish millions in profits and abuse of data privacy can attract unwanted scrutiny and fines from regulators, while damaging reputations. Our research indicates that the direct cost of dealing with a cyber attack for a large company is on average over £330,000, and can reach over £1 million. This doesn't include the reputational or brand damage and the consequent impact on revenues. The real impact is likely to be considerably higher.

Whatever a hacker's background and motivation, if they are suitably driven and skilled, they will get into almost any network. With comprehensive cyber defence in place, a large proportion of attacks can be stopped. However, this means that those who do penetrate the network are determined or talented enough to present a serious threat, and consequently a comprehensive strategy is required to defend an organisation in the event of a breach.

The first step in the battle to mitigate damage is to be prepared. Recent research shows that only 29% of businesses have formal written cyber security policies and only 10% of businesses have a formal incident management plan.[1] For such a plan to be effective it needs to be regularly tested, with lessons identified and its measures updated and enhanced. Only half of respondents' organisations had tested their incident response plan in the previous six months.

Managing the response to a cyber incident is a complex task that involves the coordination of many resources, tasks and information. Events and threats must be understood. Decisions must be taken. Technical measures must be

---

1   https://www.gov.uk/government/uploads/system/uploads/ attachment_data/file/521465/Cyber_Security_Breaches_ Survey_2016_main_report_FINAL.pdf

deployed. Further damage must be avoided. Stakeholders must be kept informed. Evidence must be preserved. Lessons should be learned. All of this will be conducted under intense time pressure and scrutiny. Preparation before the event allows organisations to focus on their strategic response rather than being caught in the web of competing tactical decisions.

WHO SHOULD I BE WORRIED ABOUT?

Attackers fall into several categories, that we have labelled *The Unusual Suspects*.[2] Each attacker has a different motivation and is likely to require different strategies to counteract.

The categories are:

- *The Activist:* These hackers take their political, social or ecological views seriously enough to want to make a public statement out of their hack. They may not be as organised as other attackers but they will aim for maximum publicity of the breach – which will discredit the targeted organisation, as well as steal sensitive data.
- *The Getaway:* Too young to go to prison, these attackers 'get away' with a reprimand. They are likely to have basic hacking skills used to impress peers and get noticed by more serious hackers.
- *The Insider:* Difficult to identify, the Insider may be a disgruntled or negligent employee or commercial spy. Inside the organisation, they can bypass security controls, copy data removable media or drives or install malware.

---

2   http://www.baesystems.com/en-uk/feature/the-unusual-suspects

- **The Mule:** A casual criminal or opportunist, the mule is used by others to launder the proceeds of a hack. The most vulnerable to detection and arrest, the mule turns cyber crime into 'real money'.

- **Nation State Actor:** Often working for a business that is bankrolled by or connected to those in power. Goes to great lengths to cover their tracks and can severely inhibit organisations.

- **The Professional:** Works at what looks like a '9 to5' job, but is a risk-averse career hacker. They may run a botnet, be part of a criminal cyber gang or sell cyber crime tools to others.

Each of these attacker profiles presents different risks to an organisation and are likely to demand different strategies to deal with them. Types of attacks can range from data breaches, such as Wikileaks or Sony Pictures, financial fraud such as the recent Bangladesh Bank heist, a Distributed Denial of Service (DDOS) website attack such as the BBC experienced or simpler malware attacks. Any incident response readiness strategy must account for multiple perpetrators and scenarios and deal with each appropriately.

FAIL TO PREPARE, PREPARE TO FAIL

"When a successful cyber-attack occurs and the scale and impact of the breach comes to light, the first question customers, shareholders, and regulators will ask is, 'What did this institution do to prepare?'" - Mckinsey[3]

---

3   http://www.mckinsey.com/business-functions/business-technology/our-insights/how-good-is-your-cyberincident-response-plan

There is no one-size-fits-all incident response readiness strategy – no two incidents or organisations are exactly the same. The response plan must be tailored to each organisation and consider a variety of incidents as well as types of attackers.

In order to be able to respond to the full range of cyber attacks, organisations should adopt a comprehensive strategy that covers the approach to: People, Process, Tools and Awareness.

PEOPLE

- *Authority:* Clearly assign roles and responsibilities for key executives accountable for managing the incident. Include escalation routes, board sponsorship and communications schedules. Consider the impact of making business critical decisions; the nominated executives must have the knowledge and experience to implement changes to critical business systems. Board level sponsorship is crucial for success of the overall plan.
- *Resource:* Ensure the right skills are available, regardless of the time or day of the week – hackers don't just work to a 9-5 timetable. Don't be overwhelmed by the attack – ensure additional resources are accessible to handle day-to-day tasks to keep the business running. It's important to maintain business as usual as far as possible. Sometimes hackers can carry out diversionary tactics by setting off one smaller hack on the network that diverts all the resource and attention, while the hacker attempts a much bigger attack elsewhere. Third party specialists can help with monitoring complex scenarios or if there is a surge of simultaneous attacks.
- *Practice:* As well as adopting a thorough incident response readiness plan, conduct regular incident response rehearsals

and penetration testing. Test exercises in crisis response handling should be co-ordinated across the organisation – from IT to HR, communications, finance and PR – and ensure that the complexity of decisions required in the event of an attack are understood. Simulating a real event will help to build awareness and experience within the team, increasing their effectiveness when a breach occurs.

PROCESS

- *Process:* Make this defined and accessible to everyone across the business. One of the main shortfalls of an incident response strategy can be the failure to communicate the plan across the business before an attack. Include guidelines and checklists and regularly re-evaluate them to ensure relevance. Another area for failure is siloed strategies, especially in global businesses. Business units often develop their own incident response plans; these work well in highly targeted attacks but are unhelpful during sustained company-wide incidents.

- *Legal:* Legal consultation may be required during an incident. Maintain data logs and adapt processes in accordance with law enforcement, particularly relevant for internal breaches where logs would be required as part of an insurance claim or court proceedings. Specific data may be required to prove an employee is violating contractual obligations in order to terminate employment. If the attack is in the public domain, evidence may be required to reassure customers and other stakeholders that all actions were taken to mitigate against risk and appropriate procedures were carried out once the attack occurred.

- *Reporting:* Damage limitation is not confined to the network and ICT systems. Construct a hierarchy of organisations, stakeholders and customers that need to be informed of the breach, including the media. Senior management will require extensive knowledge of the attack to ensure the correct information is relayed at the right time. Regulators may also require information following an attack; for example telecommunications companies are required by law to disclose any information regarding a data breach. Even for organisations that are not legally bound to publically declare an attack the reputational damage of failing to declare a breach that is subsequently made public can be significant. A clear reporting process can avoid many of these issues.

TOOLS

* *Evidence:* Maximise logging with sufficient storage on all devices, such as firewalls, proxies and active directory servers. If an attack is suspected, then avoid installing new software to collect data as it could alert the attackers and cause them to conduct diversionary tactics. Additionally, don't take infected machines offline until the threat is fully understood – this evidence may be required should the case go to court, or for other litigation or regulatory reasons.
* *Investigation:* Devise a priority matrix to help triage and understand the *who*, *what*, *when*, *why* and *how* of the attack. Consider all possibilities, discovery of unknown unknowns and the root cause of the attack to defend against attacks elsewhere on the network. Verify what has been taken without making any assumptions. Network and disk forensics as well as malware analysis and attribution can assist, as well as third party forensics teams.
* *Remediation:* Applying remedial actions across the estate should be done as rapidly as possible – with risks

weighed up for more drastic actions, such as website or network closures – if necessary. Take into consideration any evidence required and the ability of the organisation to continue business as usual. Closely monitor the corrective actions to ensure success – it is likely that a hacker may have been inside the organisation for weeks or even months and therefore is unlikely to simply accept being locked out. They may see responses as a challenge and take action to implement even more damage. Instigate recovery from backups where required and ensure constant and consistent oversight of the networks to prevent repeat attacks.

Awareness

- **Threat Aware:** Intelligence related to the attack methods and perpetrator can be used to initiate the appropriate response, improve remediation tactics and understand the severity of an attack. Adapt the response to the typical threat behaviours for more rapid recovery. The *Cyber Security Breaches* survey states viruses, spyware and malware are the most common forms of attack at 68% with impersonation of organisations at 32%, so devise strategies for these threats first.

- **Impact Aware:** The business implications of an attack can be devastating, not just on the organisation that is breached, but on customers, supply chains and stakeholders. Evaluate the impact of business critical decisions while minimising the impact of the attack. For example, if networks are taken offline, what is the risk to the rest of the business, how many staff are able to function, and what is the risk to customers and profits?

- **Context Aware:** Sophisticated hackers conduct reconnaissance about when sensitive information such as financial statements or new product launches are due for release. The hackers may have infiltrated the network for months before they attack, which will give them the potential to cause the most damage. Increase awareness of specific targets and times of greater sensitivity, and enhance monitoring and detection capabilities to mitigate against the risk of an attack.

Establishing and communicating an incident response readiness strategy will reduce the opportunity for mistakes, limit the impact of an attack and ensure greater chance of the right evidence being available, should it be required.

EXECUTING THE STRATEGY AFTER AN ATTACK

Figure 5.1.2

The first hours after an incident has been detected are the most critical. Whether alerted by an anti-virus alert, a tip off from an external party or suspected inside activity, the response should be immediate. It can be perilous to ignore anything that concerns possible cyber attacks.

The immediate aftermath is the best opportunity to capture data about the hack and use this threat intelligence to ensure the appropriate response is coordinated effectively. With an incident response plan in place, execution becomes a more strategic and less frantic job.

We recommend a five step execution plan, characterised by the image in Figure 5.1.2, as part of the emergency response in the immediate hours after detecting a breach.

Step 1: Confirm

Before escalating the incident, verify all the information available at the time without making assumptions. What is the status of the network and what, if any, data has been accessed? Immediate action must be taken to protect the remaining data and network while simultaneously ensuring evidence is preserved. Mitigate as much risk as possible at this early stage and assess the risk versus benefits to any major network decisions. Consider whether escalation is required at this stage, including management of media and stakeholders.

Step 2: Capture

Ensure all evidence of the breach is recorded by maximising logging on multiple devices across the network. Explore the incident, particularly if specific stolen data appears online. Gathering as much data as possible in the early stages can deliver threat intelligence and help dictate the effectiveness of the response. At this stage third party experts may be called upon to deploy network probes and host agent software to give remote access to the network and help gather evidence.

Step 3: Expose

The full range of discovery techniques should be applied, such as forensic tools, behavioural log analysis and reverse malware engineering. It is crucial to understand who is conducting the attack, whether it is a group, a state or an individual; where the attack is coming from, internally or externally, and what the attackers did while inside the network, including any data that has been taken or exposed online. Fully briefing board members and informing the media is appropriate at this stage. Don't under or overplay the scenario, keep to the facts and remediation techniques being deployed to overcome the situation.

Step 4: Remediate

With the intelligence already gathered and analysed, the most effective method for inhibiting the attack and recovering the infected components should be deployed. This may not be the most drastic action available, and could simply be the removal of the malware while maintaining current systems. If an insider attack has occurred it could be to take the suspected individual offline and investigate further before blocking them from the network.

Step 5: Resume

Continue to monitor the network for further attacks and to ensure the hacker has been removed. Scrutinise social networks in the aftermath for any new data and consider inspecting outside networks, such as the cloud networks used by hackers to dump information, to ensure no further data leakages occur. Review the incident response readiness plan and adapt according to lessons learned.

CONCLUSION

There are two types of organisation: those that know they have been hacked and those who don't. With the average time taken to detect a breach now at more than 100 days, this observation has never been truer.

Despite the best efforts from the world's best security teams, breaches occur and data is regularly exposed. There is no silver bullet when it comes to handling an incident, internal or external. The winners in this war will be the ones who prevent an attack as much as possible in the first instance, detect the hack as early as possible and have a cast-iron strategy for rapid response and damage limitation.

5.2

EVERYONE THINKS THEY HAVE A PLAN

Kevin Duffey, Cyber Rescue Alliance

Successful CEOs are exploiting the digital economy to continue to innovate and grow. At the same time they have to develop their organisational resilience against growing cyber risks that threaten their reputation and continued success.

Typically, an information breach is discovered many weeks after the hackers first compromised your systems. And in more than half of major breaches, the CEO learns about the breach from the police, a customer, or from some other person outside their organisation. CEOs then wish they had a plan, or at least a decision framework, as they will be making urgent choices based on crisis updates that may be incomplete and unreliable.

By definition, an online attack is different from a fire or any physical crisis, in that you can't see it. And when responding to what may be a catastrophic breach, the leader is constantly playing catch-up, not just with the hackers, but often with customers, staff, the media, regulators, partners and others. This chapter outlines the critical dos and don'ts when a cyber crisis occurs. It is based on real-life examples and scenarios that are relevant across all industry sectors.

CHALLENGES FACED BY A CEO DURING A CYBER ATTACK

CEOs want to protect their reputations and revenues by making effective decisions during the cascade of commercial consequences that can follow a catastrophic cyber attack. During the "Golden Hour" after a major breach, they need their executives to be resilient to the shock and ambiguity of the breach. CEOs need their teams to avoid instinctive responses that may be well intentioned, but can exacerbate the situation. In short, CEOs want to be ready for the low probability – but very high impact – consequences of a major breach.

We have summarised the seven challenges faced by a CEO during a catastrophic cyber attack below:

1. **The shock** to your leaders is made worse by several factors. For example, they may be told of this breach by an outsider, most frequently by law enforcement (41%) or third parties including customers (35%). They may then discover they weren't told of previous data incidents. Even worse, they're weeks behind the attackers,[4] as the average time to discover a breach is 69 days (followed by 70 days of technical containment[5]).
2. **Help from authorities** is easier if you already have some relationships with the right people. But who? For example, there are 31[6] organisations fighting cyber threats to financial services in the UK, but many are little

---

4   http://www.cyberrescue.co.uk/library/response
5   http://www.cyberrescue.co.uk/library/threat
6   Ibid

known. For example, 68%[7] of Directors are unaware even of Action Fraud.[8]

Some authorities have fewer resources than they'd like. For example, the ICO[9] has 30 officers handling over 200,000 concerns and 1,000 cases per year. Only 4%[10] of cyber crime is dealt with appropriately by the police.

3. **The chain of command** will be challenged by ambiguity during a suspected breach. We all like facts: sadly in the event of a serious breach the only fact will be that you won't know all the facts. Opinions may fill the gap where facts are missing. Only 45%[11] of security professionals are confident they can determine the scope of a breach. External forensics typically lasts 43[12] days. And decisions must be made fast: 91%[13] of consumers expect effective communications within 24 hours or less of a public attack.

4. **Your legal and moral responsibilities** might not be immediately clear. For example, law enforcement may ask you not to notify customers, so that the hacker won't be alerted to their investigations.

Extra-territorial laws on protection of citizens from cyber attack mean you may be subject to the requirements of more countries than you operate in. Just a summary of international Privacy & Breach Notification laws runs to 425 pages.[14]

---

7   Ibid

8   http://www.cyberrescue.co.uk/suppliers/authorities

9   http://www.cyberrescue.co.uk/library/response

10   https://www.linkedin.com/pulse/banks-hide-cyber-attacks-says-uk-police-kevin-duffey

11   http://www.cyberrescue.co.uk/library/threat

12   http://www.cyberrescue.co.uk/library/response

13   http://www.cyberrescue.co.uk/library/threat

14   http://www.cyberrescue.co.uk/library/response

5. **Serious decisions require money.** In the UK, 52%[15] of CEOs think they have cyber insurance, but less than 10% actually do. Some 81%[16] of companies with cyber cover in USA have never claimed on their policies. Claims paid have been on: crisis services (78%[17]); legal defence (8%) and settlement (9%).

Will you pay for a big gesture? 53%[18] of breach notifications offer credit monitoring. And what will be the long term revenue impact? Abnormal churn[19] after a breach ranges from 6.2% in financial services and 5.3% in health, down to 0.1% in the public sector.

6. **The surge** in enquiries can quickly turn into even more irate calls from customers who – in *their* moment of crisis – want to receive the global standard in call centre response: 80% of calls answered in 20 seconds.[20]

But after a breach, call volumes can be one hundred times higher than normal and in addition, you must communicate with regulators, suppliers, the Press, staff, police and shareholders, and manage the social media.

7. **The company will be criticised** even if your organisation suffered a criminal attack. Customers complain that you notified them "too slowly … too fast … without cause … putting us at risk of scammers." Consumers might say, "Credit monitoring doesn't help me" or "How will you make this good?" or simply, "I want to break my contract and leave."

---

15 http://www.cyberrescue.co.uk/suppliers/insurance

16 Ibid

17 http://www.cyberrescue.co.uk/library/threat

18 http://www.cyberrescue.co.uk/library/response

19 http://www.cyberrescue.co.uk/library/threat

20 https://www.talkdesk.com/blog/call-center-performance-benchmarks/

To assist Boards and their executive management teams to appreciate these challenges and how they plan for and test a better incident response to the crisis as and when it occurs, cyber simulations have often been highly successful. They will help you avoid the animal instincts that can overwhelm, leading well intentioned professionals to take actions with very negative consequences.

TYPICAL INSTINCTS

With apologies to Aesop, here are the instincts we've found to be typical:

HEDGEHOG   *The Hedgehog invests in breach defence, but has no strategy if defences fail.*

Frequency: This is a common problem. For example, less than 10% of large companies have any cyber insurance, according to a government report in March 2015.

Impact: Poor response to a data breach erodes sympathy. Clients and suppliers may consider suing you. The media will be critical, regulators may consider fines, investors and other stakeholders may lose confidence in your business.

OSTRICH   *The Ostrich keeps its head in the sand, denying it has suffered a data breach until the evidence is overwhelming.*

Frequency: Very often a company can't tell what data was taken. Cisco reports that half of IT specialists don't believe they could determine the scope of a data breach.

Impact*: This instinct brings significant risks, both reputational and direct. If a breach becomes public months after it occurred, you could be accused of putting your business reputation ahead of the welfare of your customers and staff.*

FROG   *The "slowly boiled Frog" gets used to "non-sensitive" incidents, and doesn't recognise or report a major breach.*

Frequency*: Incident fatigue is common among IT professionals who see daily attacks on your network. 55% of CEOs aren't told about data breaches in their company.*

Impact*: If executives aren't alerted to a breach, consequences may be ignored until too late. These include regulatory, legal, business continuity, stakeholder, consumer, employee morale and other reputational impacts.*

HARE   *The Hare identifies a breach, and in its rush to respond, trips over itself.*

Frequency*: It is rare, and happens when a senior executive has a "hero complex," or simply wants to do the right thing but is not adequately trained and experienced.*

Impact*: "Tripping up" could mean turn-ing off computers before forensics can investigate, announcing a "breach" that doesn't require notification, or starting notifications before being ready to deal with disgruntled customers.*

SNAIL   *The Snail identifies a breach, but then fails to act quickly enough.*

Frequency*: This is common if the potential business impact of the breach isn't recognised.*

Impact*: Failure to act quickly can be used against an organisation by media, lawyers, regulators, suppliers, customers and others. The breach may be made public before your organisation has prepared its response, e.g. by hackers, media or customers.*

GIRAFFE   *The Giraffe looks down on a breach, and declares that the consequences aren't significant, for most of its consumers, partners and staff.*

Frequency*: This is fairly common when only a small part of the data held is known to have been breached, and if the main concern is short term share price.*

Impact*: If a company announces a breach "only affects a few of our customers," it irritates those customers enormously, and risks a negative narrative in the media.*

TIGER   *A Tiger is solitary, and thinks it can respond to a breach on its own.*

Frequency*: This is common, especially among large organisations.*

Impact*: Large companies have lots of skilled staff. But during a major cyber attack, the tiger discovers that it has failed to develop relationships, for example with media proxies (experts who can complement your company), forensic and operational experts, law enforcement, and customers who may be impacted.*

DECISION MAKING

Making sensible decisions at speed can prove critical to minimising the harm from a successful cyber attack and in recovering effectively. Organisations should learn lessons that– sadly – many other organisations have learnt the hard way. Any effective response will be multi-layered, involving multiple stakeholders across the organisation – there are key questions the board and crisis response team will need to ask themselves:

- What is our Command and Control for this event?
- How can we best protect our customers' interests?
- How can we minimise reputational damage?
- How can we protect shareholder trust?
- What will be the impact on our most precious information and how has the attack impacted our ability to do business, now and in the future?
- What changes do we need to make to our operating practices and management processes to ensure we don't have to deal with another crisis?

Those organisations that have experience in guiding an organisation through a crisis typically summarise the challenge into three main areas:

1. **Plan, plan, plan:** Having a distinct and appropriate plan to deal with a significant data breach is essential. This plan will clearly lay out the questions, a typical timeline for the crisis, the different communications requirements and the wide variety of scenarios you may have to deal with.
2. **Rehearse:** Similar to having a plan for a fire, there is no point in having a plan unless you regularly test and adapt your response to a crisis. Those who test crisis scenarios in

a mock simulation and subsequently update plans tend to perform better.

3. **Collaborate and integrate:** A significant data breach will rely on effective collaboration across multiple teams, who prior to a crisis all know what their role is and how they will work together in a high stress environment.

CONCLUSIONS

In the wake of many high profile cyber breaches it is vital that business leaders also concentrate on decreasing the risk of attack as well as designing and testing their response and recovery plan as and when an attack occurs. There are some important questions any board should know the answers to:

- Do we have a cyber resilience strategy and does it support our agreed business strategy?
- Do we understand what and how we are investing in protecting our most valuable information, – including that which we have outsourced to our partners and suppliers?
- Do we have an effective information security awareness learning programme in place across our organisation?
- Do we have a well-defined, tried and tested incident response plan in the event of a significant data breach?
- Have we established an appropriate cyber risk escalation framework that includes our risk appetite and reporting thresholds?

Of course, the need to prevent breaches in the first instance becomes even more apparent after a catastrophic cyber attack has been simulated. With cyber attacks now targeting and threatening our most sensitive and valuable information, forgetting is sadly no longer an option. Ignorance is no longer a defence. The risks and impacts are too great.

The great majority of breaches are caused by human error – the unwitting actions of anyone in an organisation, regardless of their role or responsibility. Engaging and relevant awareness learning for all staff that provides them with the simple, practical guidance they need to make the right decisions at the right time can prove to be the most cost effective defence against attacks.

LEARNING IS KEY

In this vital area of staff training and development, one size doesn't fit all. The current "all staff, once a year" approach, simply does not influence or change behaviours. At best, it reminds us of some essentials; at worst, it's treated as unnecessary, a distraction and as something I have to do . . . or else. Annual e-learning will not instil and sustain the cyber resilient behaviours that employees need today. We're trying to "programme" our people in the same way we programme computers to do certain things, in defined ways at certain times. This approach doesn't work with people.

Instead, there needs to be a range of learning techniques that truly engage all our people, embedding and sustaining the resilient behaviours required to more effectively protect an organisation's most sensitive and valuable information and systems.

All organisations are at risk from having the fundamentals of their business undermined from a cyber attack; without effective planning and testing to cope with a crisis they could be facing a catastrophic crisis. As Warren Buffet once said: "It takes 20 years to build a reputation and 5 minutes to ruin it. If you think about that, you'll do things differently".

5.3

MANAGING A CYBER INCIDENT

Sam Millar and Helen Vickers, DLA Piper UK

Unfortunately, cyber-attackers do penetrate even the most robust and well-implemented cyber security defences. Therefore, an essential part of any cyber security strategy is preparation in the event of a cyber incident. A detailed cyber incident response plan which has been subject to penetration testing is essential. This should detail clear lines of responsibility and steps to be taken in the event of a cyber attack. All employees should be trained on the incident response plan. This chapter sets out best practice strategies for dealing with a cyber security incident (based on experience over a number of years involving incidents in the Financial Services, Energy and Gambling sectors), all of which should be codified into a cyber incident response plan.

RESPONSE

IDENTIFY

A business' immediate response to a cyber attack is crucial – it can either go a long way to mitigate potential damage or worsen the situation. The first step is to identify the scope and extent of the attack.[21] Businesses will want to understand exactly which systems, networks and assets have been compromised. At this point, an internal security incident triage process can begin to classify the severity of the cyber incident and assign it to appropriate personnel, dependent on the severity of the incident.[22]

ASSEMBLE A TEAM

An incident response team must be swiftly assembled on the discovery of a cyber incident. This will be an internal team who will coordinate the management of the cyber incident. Ideally, roles and responsibilities will have been clearly delineated in the incident response plan and so team members will be able to hit the ground running in the event of an incident. The incident response team should include key management stakeholders who are able to coordinate the business' response to the incident. There should also be a management point of contact to liaise with external resource.[23] If the business which is the victim of a cyber attack is a small business, it may not have sufficient resources to assemble an internal incident response team. Instead, it could designate a first responder – ideally someone with business decision capability. That first responder would contact and coordinate external assistance whilst remaining the main point of contact for the incident response.[24] Consider involving an internal or

---

21   CREST, *Cyber Incident Response Guide*, 2013, p. 35

22   CREST, *Cyber Incident Response Guide*, 2013, p. 36

23   PWC, *Cyber Security Crisis Management*, 2014 p. 15

24   Cyber Security Coalition, *Cyber Security Incident Management Guide*, 2015, p. 12

external lawyer. Mitigating the risks of litigation arising from the incident must be a key consideration and engaging a lawyer may enable businesses to attain legal privilege over communications created during aspects of the investigation which would otherwise be disclosable in a legal action.

CONTAIN THE INCIDENT

Once a cyberattack has been discovered, businesses will want to limit the damage, stop the attacker and prevent the incident from spreading any further. If the attack is discovered whilst it is still ongoing, there is an important strategic decision to be made at the outset: disconnect the systems to resume business as soon as possible or take the time to collect evidence against the cyber-criminal who attacked the system?[25] Disconnecting the systems will jeopardise the effectiveness of any investigation because it alerts the cyber-criminal to their discovery. However, it is the fastest way back to business as usual and it can limit the extent of the attack as the attacker is in the system for less time.[26] Immediately shutting down the server without first ensuring that the RAM is dumped onto a USB drive will destroy crucial evidence.[27] On the other hand, choosing to observe the cyber-attacker allows the affected business to gather significantly more evidence and means it is more likely to be able to tackle the root causes of the problem

---

25   Cyber Security Coalition, *Cyber Security Incident Management Guide*, 2015, p. 22

26   Cyber Security Coalition, *Cyber Security Incident Management Guide*, 2015, p. 22

27   Cyber Security Coalition, *Cyber Security Incident Management Guide*, 2015, p. 14

through an investigation. However, it will take longer to resume normal business operations.[28]

As discussed in previous chapters, there are myriad types of cyber attack and the above decision making process may not apply to all of these. If the attack in question involves an insider stealing sensitive information, the business will have to consider which 'quick wins' it can implement to mitigate the damage; for example, changing the system passwords if the system has been compromised. If the attack took place in a critical business area, the business may wish to clear the area to allow for evidence to be gathered and implement temporary access restrictions whilst the investigation is underway.

ERADICATION

Once the attacker has been stopped and the incident contained, the attack must be eradicated from the system. All components related to the incident should be removed and all holes/vulnerabilities which were exploited by the hacker should be closed. It is important not to do this until there is a full picture of the incident.[29]

RECOVERY

Once the attack has been eradicated from the system, businesses will want to start thinking about the recovery of the systems affected. The incident response plan should have a recovery element to it – guidelines which cover rebuilding infected systems, replacing compromised files, removing

---

28   Cyber Security Coalition, *Cyber Security Incident Management Guide*, 2015, p. 22

29   Cyber Security Coalition, *Cyber Security Incident Management Guide*, 2015, p. 24

temporary constraints and resetting passwords.[30] Businesses may have a business continuity plan which enables recovery of systems quickly through back-up available on un-connected systems.

INSURANCE

Businesses should consider taking out cyber insurance as a strategy to mitigate cyber risk. Cyber insurance covers the losses relating to damage to or loss of information from IT systems and networks.[31] Cyber insurance is a developing phenomenon which is becoming increasingly popular, particularly amongst the retail, airline and FS sectors. Businesses should analyse the policy wording carefully to understand the coverage the policy will provide. Some policies will provide a ready-made incident response team – this may be particularly useful for small businesses with limited resources. The benefits of cyber-insurance are relatively untested as the market is still evolving; however, a "herd mentality" means that its popularity is on the rise.

INVESTIGATION

Once a cyber attack has been discovered and the immediate response has contained and eradicated the threat, the investigation will begin. The investigation will involve examining how the attacker was able to penetrate the system and gathering evidence. The gathering of evidence may include deep-dive forensics into the systems which were

---

30   Cyber Security Coalition, *Cyber Security Incident Management Guide*, 2015, p. 25

31   https://www.abi.org.uk/Insurance-and-savings/Products/Business-insurance/Cyber-risk-insurance

affected and interviewing employees. If appropriate, the business may wish to contact law enforcement agencies.

INTERNAL INVESTIGATION

Businesses should consider whether they have sufficient resources to conduct an internal investigation or whether they require external assistance. The main advantage of investigating the incident in-house is cost – internal resources are significantly cheaper than engaging third parties. However, depending on the scale of the breach and the size of the business, it may not be possible to investigate the incident entirely in-house and so elements of the investigation may have to be outsourced. There may also be a need for independence, depending on the nature of the investigation.

EXTERNAL INVESTIGATION

The benefit of hiring counsel to conduct an investigation is that the investigation and the report of the investigation will be privileged. Legal privilege in England and Wales means that a party can withhold certain categories of documents from production to a third party or the court.[32] Legal advice privilege applies to confidential communications between a lawyer and a client and all materials forming part of the continuum of those communications.[33] Privilege can be waived – either expressly by the client consenting to a

---

32 http://globalinvestigationsreview.com/article/1036098/ investigations-and-legal-privilege-the-price-of-your-human-rights

33 The Law Society, *Legal Professional Privilege: The Law Society Guidance on its Usage*, 26 July 2016, p. 2

limited disclosure of certain privilege information, or by the inadvertent disclosure of privileged information.[34]

There has been some controversy around legal privilege in investigations, with regulatory authorities taking issue with the use of privilege in internal investigations. Jamie Symington (Director of Enforcement [wholesale, unauthorised business and intelligence] at the FCA) in a speech in November 2015 stated that firms relying on legal advice privilege to protect notes of initial interviews is a *"'gaming' of the process in order to shroud the output of an investigation in privilege."*[35] Mr Symington went on to say that *"where firms propose to carry out or commission an internal investigation themselves – the starting point is that we expect them to share the core product of their investigation – i.e. the evidence – with us."*[36] Furthermore, the Enforcement Guide in the FCA Handbook goes so far as to state that: *"It is for the firm to decide whether to provide such material to the FCA. But a firm's willingness to volunteer the results of its own investigation, whether protected by legal privilege or otherwise, is welcomed by the FCA and is something the FCA may take into account when deciding what action to take, if any."*

In response, the Law Society published a consultation paper on legal professional privilege in July 2016. Whilst the paper is still in the consultation stage at the time of writing, it set out the view that *"adverse inferences cannot be drawn from a client's refusal to waive LPP, no regulator*

---

34 The Law Society, *Legal Professional Privilege: The Law Society Guidance on its Usage*, 26 July 2016, p. 5

35 https://www.fca.org.uk/news/speeches/internal-investigations-by-firms-

36 https://www.fca.org.uk/news/speeches/internal-investigations-by-firms-

or investigator is entitled to pressure a client to waive LPP and in such circumstances it is for the regulator to decide whether the client should in some way be credited if it takes that decision".[37]

If the cyber investigation is undertaken for a client with regulatory reporting obligations, it will be for the client to decide the extent to which it will share evidence of its privileged internal investigation with its regulator. What the Law Society makes clear is that the regulator is not in a position to pressure the client to do so. Clients should carefully consider when conducting an investigation with external counsel whether a document in question needs to be created or whether a conversation would be equally effective. Similarly, internal documents analysing the commercial impact of the incident should be kept to a minimum.

THIRD PARTY FORENSICS

Businesses may wish to appoint a third-party forensic expert to assist with the investigation of the cyber incident. The ideal forensic partner is one with the technical expertise to carry out the investigation of a sophisticated security incident quickly and effectively.

There are several advantages to using third party forensic experts. They are able to provide resource and expertise, through experienced staff who understand how to carry out cyber investigations. A forensic partner should be able to conduct the investigation from a technical perspective, using their technical knowledge to perform deep-dive forensic analysis. Furthermore, they can perform a cyber security analysis which will allow the business to continue to monitor

---

37   The Law Society, *Legal Professional Privilege: The Law Society Guidance on its Usage*, 26 July 2016, p. 7

its cyber threats.[38] Their experience and familiarity with such investigations means that their investigatory techniques will avoid comprising any evidence.

Whilst businesses may reach the conclusion that a forensic expert would be helpful to the investigation, they may find it difficult to choose one. It is advisable to build a list of contacts, including third-party forensic experts, into any incident response plan so that the experts can quickly and easily be contacted in the event of an incident. Businesses should consider the location of the investigation and question whether they need a forensic vendor with international reach and the ability to deploy teams globally, or whether a local forensic vendor would be sufficient.

In the UK, CREST has collaborated with the UK Government to develop the CESG/CPNI Cyber Incident Response service, launched in August 2013. This service is twofold, involving both a scheme focused on maintaining an appropriate standard for cyber incident response, as well as a smaller government-run cyber incident response scheme certified by CESG and CPNI using specialist industry partners to respond to cyber attacks. This is intended to enable victims of cyber attacks to source an appropriate third-party forensic vendor suitable for their needs. Both elements of the scheme will include an introduction of mandated cyber professional qualifications.[39]

COMMUNICATION

A crucial element of any cyber security investigation is the communications plan. Communication will be essential throughout the investigation of a cyber incident – from

---

38 CREST, *Cyber Incident Response Guide*, 2013, p. 47
39 CREST, *Cyber Incident Response Guide*, 2013, p. 47

discovery to resolution. A PR strategy and communications plan should be integrated into the cyber incident response plan. It is advisable to have someone from the PR/communications department on the incident response team. Businesses should establish who the key stakeholders are and what information they need; for example, the media, the customers and the regulator.[40] A good basic rule is to communicate on a "need to know" basis only.[41] This will avoid a situation whereby information is unnecessarily disseminated amongst parties for whom it may do more harm than good to be 'in the loop'. Once the business has established who will be informed and what they will be informed of, they should determine when is the best point to share the information.

An effective communications plan should be deployed early in the process so as to control the narrative in the media. However, there is a balance to be struck between transparency and evaluation. Sometimes it may be better to wait until the full fact pattern has emerged, particularly for customers whose data has been affected. It is often worse to have to contact customers several times with different information.[42] TalkTalk initially warned all 4 million of its customers that they may have been affected by the data breach, sparking panic amongst investors and customers and sending TalkTalk's share price down by almost a third overnight. It eventually transpired that only 156,000 customers had been affected.[43]

Businesses which are regulated may have mandatory

40   Cyber Security Coalition, *Cyber Security Incident Management Guide*, 2015, p. 16

41   Cyber Security Coalition, *Cyber Security Incident Management Guide*, 2015, p. 26

42   PWC, *Cyber Security Crisis Management*, 2014, p. 13

43   City AM, *Make it Mandatory for firms to report all data breaches*: TalkTalk boss, Billy Bambrough, 28 July 2016

regulatory reporting obligations which they have to adhere to.[44] For example, energy companies must report interruption data to the regulator Ofgem as part of a reliability incentive scheme.[45] Depending on the nature of the breach, companies may also consider reporting the breach to the ICO. Although there is no legal obligation on data controllers to do so, the ICO advises that serious data breaches should be reported. Telecoms providers and internet service providers must notify the ICO of a data breach within 24 hours of becoming aware of the essential facts of the breach. The Chief Executive of TalkTalk has gone so far as to call for the mandatory reporting of all data breaches.[46] The GDPR will include the power for regulators to levy heavy financial sanctions of up to 4% of an annual worldwide turnover of an organisation for privacy non-compliance.[47]

POST-INCIDENT REVIEW

The final part of any cyber investigation should be a review of the incident management process. Businesses must examine how effective each element of the cyber incident response plan was. Questions should be asked around the communications plan, the personnel chosen to implement each part of the response, the cooperation of management, whether anything prevented a swift recovery and whether the plan was adequate. Cyber threats are constantly evolving and as such businesses must be sure to review and update all aspects of their security framework, in particular, their cyber

---

44 Please note that this is not intended to be an exhaustive guide.

45 CREST, *Cyber Incident Response Guide*, 2013, p. 43

46 City AM, Make it Mandatory for firms to report all data breaches: TalkTalk boss, Billy Bambrough, 28 July 2016

47 For further information, please see chapter 1.8.

incident response plans to ensure that, as far as possible, the same weaknesses cannot be exploited again.

GOVERNMENT GUIDANCE

The UK government has produced various guidance relating to cyber security, as well as accreditation schemes and standards. These are resources which businesses can draw on to assist them in their development of a robust security system and incident management planning.

The government-backed Cyber Essentials Scheme means that businesses can be independently certified if they meet a good practice standard in their cyber security measures. The scheme requires businesses to enact basic technical controls over five areas: (i) boundary firewalls and internal gateways, (ii) secure configurations, (iii) user access controls, (iv) malware protection and (v) patch management. The survey found that half of all firms said they already had the controls in place to a sufficient standard to be certified but had not realised that the certification was available.[48]

The more time businesses invest in building a successful cyber security framework, the more effective their defences will be in the event of an attack. A cyber incident response plan is a fundamental part of this cyber security framework. The response plan should be subject to testing and regular updating to ensure that it can be effectively mobilised in the event of an incident. A well thought-out cyber incident response plan, allocating clear lines of responsibility and an effective communications plan, will not stop a cyber attack but will assist in mitigating its effects.

---

48   HM Government and Ipsos MORI, *2016 Cyber Security Breaches Survey 2016*, May 2016, p. 13

5.4

TURBULENCE AND FURTHER THREATS

Steve Culp, Chris Thompson and John Narveson,
Accenture Finance & Risk Practice for Financial Services

Most firms are currently working on a better way to address cyber risk, but few have mastered it. Why? In our view, companies face at least four types of challenges:

1. Organisational silos

Cyber risk is often viewed as a technology limitation managed by security (physical or cyber), and is typically owned by the chief information security Officer (CISO). Disparities in risk ownership may lead to insufficient interaction with the chief risk officer (CRO) or with the business, thus limiting the visibility to frequency or impact.

2. Insufficient business involvement

Information security should be viewed as a business issue, not only a technology one. Companies should manage cyber security risk from a business-centric, enterprise-holistic perspective.

3. Over-reliance on training and communications

The weakest link in cyber resiliency is the human element. However, most cyber risk mitigation programmes rely too heavily on changing human behaviour as the control mechanism for cyber risk. Cyber attacks often go after the path of least resistance; however, a cyber resilient organisation is able to contain that attack and not rely solely on people as the way to mitigate or control the risk.

4. Talent shortfalls

Similar to the silos created between CRO, CISO, chief operating officer (COO) and chief information officer (CIO), talent often follows either the business or technology path, which leads to competing priorities. With high demands for technology-savvy resources, the availability of talent to build a resilient business may be limited.

A METHODOLOGY FOR BUILDING CYBER RESILIENCY

We believe that holistic capabilities across risk and security underpin the approach to defining and delivering cyber resiliency. Financial services companies need to bring together capabilities to execute risk assessments, support effective surveillance, enhance incident response and strengthen controls to become more cyber resilient.

Our recommended methodology encompasses the full breadth of entry points and angles by which financial organisations need to build readiness and cyber resilience. (See Figure 5.4.1.)

Figure 5.4.1 A Methodology for Building Cyber Resiliency

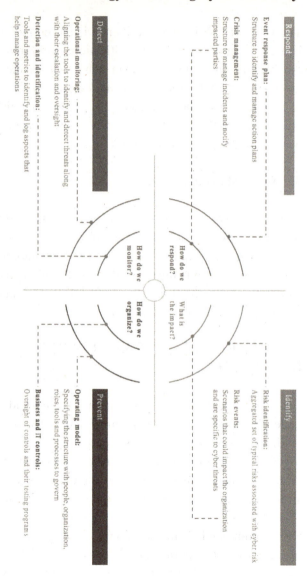

Source: How to Make Your Enterprise Cyber Resilient, Accenture, October 2015

IDENTIFICATION: WHAT IS THE IMPACT?

Organisations should develop the capability to quickly identify where a cyberattack is taking place so that they can prevent, detect and respond as necessary. What scenarios can help to proactively prevent events from happening? What are the risk mitigation strategies that a firm could put into place to address impacts before they become real?

So-called "penetration testing" has become one way to proactively identify weaknesses in a firm's cyber defence structures. We believe firms need to go beyond executing prepared scripts and move to advanced adversary impersonation. Inside and/or outside groups are hired or assigned to attempt to breach the company's defences, probing networks, applications and other computer systems. Security professionals then use that information to improve their defences.

The findings often demonstrate that the gaps and deficiencies are with the people, rather than with the technologies. Externals are able to gain access to critical information and secure areas without having to break through firewalls and other technology-based protection layers.

Better information sharing is also important. Organisations should share and have access to all threat indicators to help decrease the rate of attacks. Advanced employee training is also essential, helping them to more readily detect and be aware of cyber attacks such as phishing. With one recent high-profile hacking in the financial services industry, indications are that the hackers gained access to the firm's data by stealing the network credentials of employees with high-level IT access.

In general, efforts should be focused on preventing and mitigating attacks and breaches instead of minimising the cost of breaches after they occur.

PREVENTION: HOW DO WE ORGANIZE?

The questions at the heart of prevention include such things as: How do we control our environment? How do we establish the proper technology hygiene in terms of developing and coding systems? How do we see that proper access is in place — using things like ISO standards for how systems are developed or how they're accessed or reviewed, and also how they operate?

With an IT organisation that's very focused on development and technology innovation, how are people in their roles organised to be able to check and double-check code for vulnerabilities or use automated controls and approaches to protect those vulnerabilities?

Proper change management is essential. Before pushing code into production, security checks are made or application changes are evaluated for security-related vulnerabilities. Good training is an important start to improving prevention capabilities, though ultimately, security controls should be so robust that the employee rarely has to even think about it.

One recent Accenture initiative in Brazil assigned a team to identify potential vulnerabilities in different mobile devices. They looked at each of the banking applications that could be downloaded, and they were able to use a system that showed many vulnerabilities that existed in those applications.

DETECTION: HOW DO WE MONITOR?

Detection includes tools and metrics to identify and log aspects to manage operations. It also includes operational monitoring — aligning the tools to identify and detect threats along with their escalation and oversight.

As currently structured at most firms, surveillance is a reactive process using tools that look at past patterns to determine if a breach has occurred. For surveillance to realise its full potential as part of cyber resilience, it should become more proactive. Data from surveillance can make addressing identified vulnerabilities more proactive instead of waiting for an event to occur. We believe that a planned, systematic approach to investing in surveillance capabilities could generate significant returns, not only in terms of preventing and reducing adverse events, but in demonstrating a firm's commitment to being a stable, dependable business partner.

Firms should consider using advanced data analytics — harvesting information from new channels such as social media and their existing channels such as transaction monitoring — to help create more predictive capabilities. Firms should be able to help prevent breaches in areas identified as having a high potential for undesirable activity. Ideally, firms should be able to turn post-event investigative data and tools into preventative detection systems that utilise analytics and real-time reporting to spot deviations from behavioural norms as they occur.

Using these methods, firms could also help create increasingly sophisticated risk profiles as they attempt to pre-empt breaches. In our experience, the total cost of investing time and resources in comprehensive, preventative surveillance is often less than the cost of investing in disconnected group-by-group efforts and the results are usually better. Most banks have separate efforts in place for employee surveillance, conduct risk and cyber risk. This could be an area to combine forces and seek better results with fewer gaps, and without needing additional funding.

RESPONSE: HOW DO WE RESPOND?

In the event a cyber attack occurs, firms should have in place an event response plan — the structure to identify and manage action plans — as well as a crisis management process to manage incidents and notify impacted parties.

A response plan includes:

1. Validating that the event is taking place and mobilising the response team.
2. Putting in place the firewalls and stopgap measures to make sure the exposure isn't expanding. This requires pre-planning and regular testing.
3. Determining the timing for alerting authorities and regulators, as well as the firm's external media team.
4. Carefully managing public relations. Some firms have appeared stronger and more organised after a breach. Others have lost significant brand value.

A firm's structured approach to cyber risk analysis should span each of the lines of defence to identify the risk components and aspect of change necessary to provide better clarity to key stakeholders. For example, scenario-driven impact analysis is one important technique. This involves conducting a tabletop scenario analysis workshop to re-evaluate the financial services firm's response programme in the event of a cyber breach, in light of heightened regulatory and management concern around cyber security.

The ability to quickly quarantine affected applications, networks and systems is also an essential part of the response plan. Based upon business case scenarios, firms should conduct business and technology resiliency tests to prepare for known and unknown situations which can occur in the case of situations which require a lockdown. They also need to be able to isolate technologies and platforms that are more susceptible to vulnerabilities and losses.

Financial services organisations need to recognize the threats of cyber risk in a different way. Many have put in place thick walls to protect themselves. But the threats from a cyber event are becoming more prolific. So, although the walls are in place, the threats or activities to commit fraud or attack a firm are evolving to evade traditional measures of protection.

Organisations cannot protect themselves at all times from the myriad of potential attacks through multiple channels. So putting in place strategies, technologies and processes to build resilience – or fast recovery – is critical to operating effectively in today's connected world.

5.5

REVIEWING AND UPDATING CONTINGENCY PLANS

Richard Preece, Orkas

So you have read this book, taken notes and applied the advice to the context of your business. Surely, job done and time to start getting back to the real business of business, growth and return on investment. Alas, to paraphrase, no plan survives contact with the enemy, or in this case: the changing nature of your business and its dependencies, threats and hazards from malicious and non-malicious cyber-incidents and the latent and new vulnerabilities created by people, processes and technology.

This is the reality of the complex *systems of systems* and hyper-connectivity that the interaction of people, technology and data create, otherwise known as cyber-space or digitisation. The result is a case of *when* and not *if* a cyber based incident will take place. If it can go wrong, it probably will go wrong, not always in the way predicted and often at the least opportune time. Due to the increasing amount of a company's value being derived from cyber-space, it can lead to an amplifier effect beyond the initial incident, placing greater importance upon consequence management.

By way of simple analogy there is a *system of systems*, creating a capability for fire based risks, which covers: culture, people, policies, plans, processes, structures, information, technology and physical assets. These are linked into protective, preventative, detective, responsive and recovery measures and controls. For example, trained people ready to use fire extinguishers, alarms, muster points, calling the fire brigade, fire-insurance, forensic investigation, etc. This system of systems has developed over centuries of hard-earned experience.

So what; the fiduciary duties of the top management of companies make it increasingly unacceptable not to have the same approach for cyber-risks. In reality this means investing in planning, resourcing, budgeting and implementing a portfolio of programmes, projects and activities to review, continuously improve and change capability. This includes a team and contingency plans that are designed and prepared to be agile, so they can operate effectively against a range of potential scenarios in a complex, uncertain and ambiguous environment.

For some organisations, this approach may be a natural extension of their culture and current practices, for others it may be new and challenging. Done properly the business can become more agile and resilient, ready to mitigate the risks and seize the opportunities of cyber-space. However, done badly it can suffer material impact and even existential threat to its survival.

The aim of this chapter is therefore to provide a framework for any business to govern, invest in, review and update scenario based contingency plans, so they stay effective and efficient. This will be achieved by identifying a simple set of core questions to be addressed. From this will lead to the types of activities that need to be done and therefore built into your company's operating model. At the heart of this approach is the acceptance that cyber-incidents (malicious and non-malicious) are a case of *when* and not *if*.

WHERE TO START – WITH THE END IN MIND

Stephen Covey identified the importance of starting with the end in mind and so it is for cyber-incidents. There are really three questions that top management need to answer and to continue to ask:

1. Business growth and return on investment – do we understand where our value is and what the cyber-risk (including opportunity) is to it?;
2. Could we defend our level of preparation and response in the aftermath of a cyber-incident?; and
3. Has the situation changed?

These simple questions help top management to provide strategic alignment, leadership and culture, governance and accountability. In turn this should lead to prioritised and ongoing resourced risk management and capability. So having posed the questions, how to answer them?

Business growth and return on investment – do we understand where our value is and what the cyber-risk is to it?

To answer this question requires an understanding of context and how the business creates value first, both now and under future plans. There are many tools and techniques that can be used and applied. However, scenario and contingency planning requires leadership and culture first and foremost to be ready to challenge one another and themselves and to be clear on what is known, what is assumed, what is unknown, but can be discovered and accepting that some things will be unknowable.

Whether starting from a mature understanding or from nothing, the simplest approach is for top management to use a facilitated workshop to develop shared understanding and agreement, with a particular focus upon cyber-space. This type of activity can focus upon how value is created, in particular how cyber-space allows the company to do things better, and to do better things. For example, through increased productivity and asset utilisation; more responsive and efficient supply chains and logistics; by improving customer and employee engagement; and, or some other form, innovation. Ultimately, this should create insights into how cyber-space enables faster, better and cheaper ways for people to people (P2P); people to machine (P2M) and machine to machine (M2M) to interact and exploit information and data.

This first activity allows more strategic evaluation of what is most important to, and needs to be prioritised by, the business. This can create new insights which can be beneficial to the business as a whole, highlighting dependencies and connections which may have grown organically over time, creating a self-organised criticality. For top management it can aid their ability to understand and lead overall business strategy and execution, enabling them to make better informed trade-off judgements between opportunities and risks.

This leads to the second stage in addressing this question – to understand the risk to the value the business creates, building upon the understanding already created and developing analysis of the insights further. This can and increasingly does include the significant risk of not digitally transforming to keep up with new or existing competition, or to innovate. This in turn enables an understanding of business impact of different scenarios upon P2P, P2M, M2M and enabling data will be on the company's reputation and brand; people and stakeholders; operations and supply-chain; legal and regulatory compliance; and financial and commercial outputs, including future investability. This process therefore provides the understanding to evaluate, direct, monitor and assure strategy, risk management and investment trade-offs. It is already done by many businesses in one form or other of strategy and risk management activities. Cyber-space strategy and risks should be no different, but it is more challenging because of the complex, dynamic and ambiguous environment, cutting across traditional functional stovepipes and linkages outside the control of the company.

This analysis can then lead to the conduct of specific cyber-risk scenario events: workshops, table-top exercises and simulations, as appropriate. Scenarios should be developed which reflect the assessed threat and vulnerabilities to your company, both malicious and non-malicious, people and technically based. The events should have clear aims and objectives and most importantly the ability to capture observations and conduct analysis to identify lessons and recommendations. These can then inform wider governance, risk management and specific contingency plans.

When preparing for, conducting and assessing the results of these cyber-risk scenario events, it is important that the most likely and most dangerous types of threats and hazards are considered as a priority. Individuals and parts of the company may find this challenging based upon past experience, assumptions and cultural norms. Perhaps the two most challenging aspects of this are for those with a non-technical background to engage with the subject matter, and recognise the human dimension, especially that of the threat posed by the malicious insider. To counter this, an education package to understand the wider issues and risks is recommended before the scenario events. Equally, there needs to be clear rules of engagement, so any discussion and debate is free and open, with the event seen as an opportunity to learn first and foremost; making mistakes and problem solving as appropriate.

The aim of these activities is to enable shared understanding and discovery driven learning, whilst improving collaboration across different functions, including potentially with external stakeholders. Many of these cyber-risk scenario activities will identify areas for measures to improve prevent, protect, and detect. The results from these events can therefore support more integrated decision making, including some of the inevitable trade-offs required to achieve strategic alignment. This leads to the strategic second question and, with it, having a view of what good looks like!

What Does Good Look Like? US Supreme Court Justice Potter Stewart famously said, "I know it when I see it" when he described the threshold test for obscenity. So it is when attempting to define what good looks like to defend a business's preparation and response to cyber-incidents. So how will you answer the second strategic question?

Could we defend our level of preparation and response in the aftermath of a cyber-incident?
The first step of this has been achieved by conducting the analysis and scenario events described above, which should help identify criticality and priority for protecting different assets and value, both tangible and intangible. However, having identified value and the criticality and priority of different cyber-space assets in achieving value, it is necessary to consider the *what* if something has an impact upon achieving value.

This means developing, practising and testing contingency plans to demonstrate they are more than mere arrangements, but fit for purpose and ready to be used. In practice this means developing an agile core multi-disciplinary team, which can bring in others as required, to dynamically problem solve and execute solutions under pressure. This team, including accountable members from top management, need stable core processes and structures that can enable rapid mobilisation and action across a range of functions.

There are, therefore, a further two questions to ask of the contingency plans as they are first developed and subsequently practised, tested and continuously adapted. These questions are:

2a. How will we detect and recognise a malicious or non-malicious cyber-incident?

The nature of many cyber-scenarios is that attribution and the time of the initial occurrence of an event and its first detection can be challenging. This means the initial assessment and reporting of an event to an appropriate authority can be delayed. So the contingency plan must have a clear policy, process, people and structure, including outsourced services if appropriate, and supporting technologies, infrastructure, information and intelligence, to make this as efficient and effective as possible. This may enable proactive actions to prevent an attack or failure of some sort or to quickly contain it. However, it is more likely to be in response to an incident having being detected, possibly through information released publicly or on the dark web. A cyber-incident contingency plan timeline and actions should therefore look something like the framework in Figure 5.5.1.

Figure 5.5.1 Generic Contingency Plan Framework

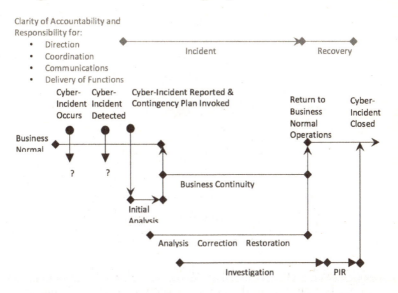

2b. Is the decision making and action process effective and ensures effective communications to stakeholders including for 2nd and 3rd order consequences?

This should be a core part of any contingency plan; it is informed by the assessment of what the incident is, but considers what the likely consequences are. The subsequent incident categorisation, which may change during an incident, should determine who has delegated responsibility for direction, coordination, action and communications.

Figure 5.5.2   Generic Incident Categorisation Framework

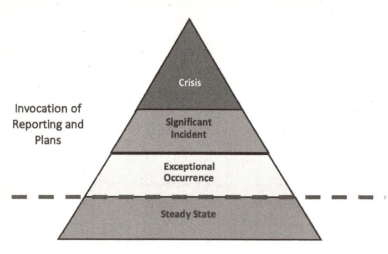

The generic incident categorisation framework in Figure 5.5.2 is a guide, but the key is to keep it simple and enable agility in execution. Any incident assessed to fit above the red dashed line should result in immediate reporting as a minimum. However, in reality there will be a routine amount of attacks and activity, which the cyber security function should understand; these should have little or no business impact and be treated as business as usual. Therefore, top management should direct what is the agreed tolerance of business impact for reporting and who should be responsible, consulted and informed, depending upon the categorisation of the incident. Ultimately a member of the top management should be accountable and ready to lead and direct the overall strategic response to a significant incident and especially a crisis.

If scenario and contingency planning have been effective, it should identify who, both internally and externally to the business, should be informed. This should be included within an incident management communications plan, which should capture *what* will be communicated, *when* it will be communicated, *with whom*, and *how*; plus any non-disclosure agreements or other caveats/factors to information sharing. This is particularly important in the event of a special investigation, often revolving around a potential malicious insider threat. Lawyers and communications specialists should help shape this plan. Stakeholders who should be considered in the plan include: employees, customers, suppliers, regulators, law enforcement, cyber information sharing portals, legal, insurance and other incident/crisis management service providers.

PULLING IT ALL TOGETHER

Cyber security and contingency planning is not simple; however, it must be done, if the fiduciary duties of the top management are to be satisfied. Therefore, it should be viewed as an essential core and ongoing business process for companies. How it is done must be driven by the top management, who must own and lead the issues and risks, although education and culture should make it everyone's responsibility to play their part. The key is to continually be ready to ask question 3.

Has the situation changed?
Ultimately contingency plans should be kept simple and have the agility to be applied to not just specific named scenarios or likely start points, but also the unexpected. They should be living documents, regularly updated following Post Incident Reviews (PIR), other organisations' lessons, development and test exercises, changes in strategy, risk appetite, personnel, technology, suppliers, intelligence and operations.

The key is to continually question assumptions and the situation. The hyper-connected (P2P, P2M and M2M) environment, in which small events can be magnified in terms of impact, means the situation is continually in flux and therefore changing. This requires a commitment, with supporting governance and accountability, risk management, leadership and culture, and agile capabilities to continually deepen and broaden individual and shared understanding of the issues and risks and to adapt. The iterative design and development review process should build upon existing company culture and processes if they already exist. As in so many things the challenge is to have sufficient detail to make the contingency plan(s) work, but not so much that it is overly prescriptive and not fit for purpose when it comes into contact with the enemy.

SUMMARY

The commercial risks of cyber invasion have proliferated and the frequency of incidents has accelerated exponentially in step with advances in IT and the pervasive use of the internet in business transactions. The number of security breaches reported to the UK Information Commissioner's Office (ICO) nearly doubled from 1,089 in 2015 to 2,048 in 2016 over a similar time period, according to a freedom of information (FOI) request by Huntsman Security. The problems are exacerbated by the time it takes for organisations to react to breaches. Verizon has revealed in its 2016 data report that while 84% of attacks compromise their selected targets within days or less, more than 75% are detected later.

Some cyber incidents on an international scale are spectacular. Until 2016 the record among reported data breaches was that of 359 million user details at My Space exposed in 2008. However, the Yahoo breach of at least 500 million users' personal details revealed this year set a new record. The most disturbing feature this time was that the breach took place in late 2014. Such breaches as these and others involving customer data in the banking sector may give a misleading impression that only large enterprises are at severe risk from invasion, but the truth is that a data breach could happen to any company at any time.

There is growing evidence in the UK that SMEs, which represent 93.3% of all private sector businesses and contribute £1.6 trillion to the economy annually, are becoming a top target for cyber-attackers; and yet 82% of SMEs still believe they are too small to be targeted. According to the Federation of Small Businesses (FSB) 92% of hacking incidents in 2014 were suffered by smaller UK companies which were targeted seven million times. The average cost of the worst breaches was estimated at £310,800 each in 2015 against £115,000 in 2014. Progressing from ignorance to awareness is a necessary first step.

THE AIMS OF THE BOOK

Managing Cyber security Risk is intended as a guide for the directors and senior management of SMEs and larger companies that have not recognised their vulnerability or taken action to address the cyber risk problem. As Jim Baines, CEO of a New York packaging company, records from his mind shifting experience in chapter 1.3, the starting point is recognition that "The leadership...of any organisation has to be actively involved in developing and setting policies; they need to proactively oversee that they are followed and updated. Above all they need to lead by example". Nor, as Don Randall emphasises in chapter 2.1 can responsibility for cyber security be shuffled off to the IT function.

For smaller companies which cannot afford a full-time Cyber Security Officer, or even suitably qualified IT Management, cyber security responsibility needs to be assumed by one Director who harnesses the processes, systems and software of one or more appropriate service providers. The book makes no attempt to identify which service offerings are the most useful or effective; there are a legion of accredited service providers, many located in Silicon

Valley, California. For those taking on their companies' cyber security responsibility with little experience, a good starting point is to follow the frequent online briefings of Tech Target (www.techtarget.com) and Computer Weekly (www.computerweekly.com) who publish in association. At the same time, advice is available from the contributors to *Managing Cyber Security Risk*, whose contact details are listed in Appendix I.

We hope that this edition of *Easy Steps to Managing Cyber Security Risk* will make a useful contribution to the wider adoption of good security practice throughout commercial enterprises.

Jonathan Reuvid
Editor

ACKNOWLEDGMENTS

The four sponsors who have made this publication possible have also contributed the greater part of the content. DLA Piper UK, the leading international law firm and a specialist in cyber security issues. Accenture, the global management consultancy. AXELOS, a joint venture co-owned between the UK government and Capita plc, has also contributed chapters from its own client experience and from its associates RSM Risk Assurance Services and the Cyber Rescue Alliance. BAE Systems Applied Intelligence has written for the final Protection and Response section of the book based on its cyber security experience in the UK defence industry. To each of these Legend Business offer its thanks for their enthusiastic participation.

As editor, I am grateful to Don Randall and Raymond Romero for their insightful chapters; also to Pauline Neville-Jones, involved in the government's cyber security initiative since its inception, who has written the Foreword to our book and has been the DRMFS keynote speaker.

APPENDIX I
CONTRIBUTORS

Chris Thompson is a Senior Managing Director, leading Accenture's Financial Services Security and Resilience Practice. Based in New York, Chris specialises in complex, large-scale finance and risk programmes. He works with some of the world's leading retail, commercial and investment banks. Chris brings 20 years of broad-based experience in financial architecture, risk management, performance management and trading to organisations determined to become high-performance businesses.

Steve Culp is Global Managing Director in Accenture's Finance & Risk Practice for Financial Services. Based in Chicago, Steve has more than 20 years of global experience working with clients to define strategy, and execute change programmes across a broad spectrum of risk management and finance disciplines. Steve is responsible for leading the global group across all dimensions, from setting the strategic direction through to the enablement of local teams operating across diverse markets. In addition, he oversees Accenture's efforts on large-scale transformation programmes across finance and risk for some of its most important financial services clients.

Jon Narveson is a Managing Director in Accenture's Finance & Risk Practice for Financial Services. Based in Charlotte, he serves as the Operational Risk Management Capability lead for North America specialising in risk identification, assessment, measurement and reporting. Jon works with major financial services institutions to develop risk-based strategies, controls and risk mitigation programmes to manage high impact and emerging risks and issues. His recent focus has included transforming operational risk management capabilities into drivers of value, profitability and sustainability, while strengthening the methods by which the risks are managed.

Accenture New York
1345 6th Avenue, New York, NY 10105
Tel: +1 917 452-8982
e-mail: chris.e.thompson@accenture.com

Nick Wilding is General Manager of Cyber Resilience at AXELOS Global Best Practice, a joint venture company set up in 2013 and co-owned by the UK Government and Capita plc, which owns and develops a number of best practice methodologies, including ITIL® and PRINCE2® used by organizations in more than 150 countries to enable them to work and operate more effectively. Nick is responsible for RESILIA™ Global Best Practice, a portfolio of cyber resilience best practice publications, certified training, staff awareness learning and leadership engagement tools designed to put the "human factor" at the centre of cyber resilience strategy, enabling effective recognition, response to and recovery from cyber attacks.

Jerome Vincent is the author of *Whaling for Beginners*, a dramatised account of a cyber attack on the CEO of a successful organisation, published by AXELOS Global Best Practice. He has been a script and copy writer for many years and has written widely about corporate technology issues for many of the world's leading multinationals.

AXELOS Global Best Practice
17 Rochester Row, London SW1P 1 QT
Tel: +44 (0) 207 960 7865
e-mail: Nick.Wilding@AXELOS.com

Julian Cracknell is Managing Director of BAE Systems Applied Intelligence UK Services business. He is responsible for client relationships and delivery across National Security, Government and the Commercial markets. Julian joined BAE Systems Applied Intelligence in 2012, initially to run the Government Client Group and then subsequently joining the board in 2013. Prior to this he worked at Logica in a number of roles including Director of National Security and Business Unit Manager for Defence Systems. His background includes the delivery of large software development programmes, commercial management and leading business development teams.

BAE Systems Applied Intelligence
Blue Fire Building, 4th Floor, 110 Southwark Street
London SE1 0TA
Tel: +44 (0) 203 296 5900
e-mail: learn@baesystems.com

Sam Millar graduated from Cambridge University (MA, Law) and the University of Illinois, USA (LLM, International and Comparative Law). He is a partner in the London office of

DLA Piper and his practice focuses on Global Investigations. Sam has extensive experience in cross border regulatory and internal corporate investigations involving allegations of cyber crime, bribery, money laundering, market abuse, fraud and insider dealing. Sam has advised clients across sectors – including financial services and energy – on cyber crime and cyber security issues. He is on the FCA's Panel of Skilled Persons for s.166 FSMA reviews relating to conduct of business.

Ben Johnson is a partner at DLA Piper specialising in financial litigation and regulatory law. His expertise in payment systems includes acting in the world's largest payment card data compromise; and he regularly now acts in engagements involving cyber crime and cyber security issues, commonly with a focus on fraud against financial institutions.

Ross McKean is a partner in the London office of DLA Piper and is the joint head of the firm's UK data protection practice. Ross is recognised as a leading international technology lawyer and advises on global data governance and compliance, information security, breach response and global sourcing projects. His clients include organisations across a wide range of sectors including retail, financial services, technology, social media, digital advertising, e-commerce, B2C SaaS and life sciences. He also advises on contentious data protection and privacy matters including information access requests and privacy group actions.

Helen Vickers graduated from Oxford University (BA, English). She is an associate in the Litigation & Regulatory Group of DLA Piper's London office. She has experience in internal corporate investigations involving allegations of financial irregularities as well as investigations involving cyber crime across a range of sectors, including financial services, retail and energy.

DLA Piper UK LLP
3 Noble Street, London EC2V 7EE
Tel: +44 (0) 207 153 7714
e-mail: Sam.Millar@dlapiper.com

Nick Ioannou is an IT professional, blogger and author with over 20 years' corporate experience, including 13 years using cloud/hosted software as a service (SaaS) systems. He started blogging in 2012 on free software and IT tips (nick-ioannou.com), currently with more than 400 posts. His first book "Internet Security Fundamentals" available at www. booleanlogical.com is an easy to understand guide of the most commonly faced security threats and criminal scams aimed at general users.

Boolean Logical Ltd
20-22 Wenlock Road, London N1 7GU
Tel: +44 (0) 780 308 5249
e-mail: nick@booleanlogical.com

Cyber IQ
IQPC, Floor 2, 129 Wilton Road, London SW1V 1JX
Tel: +44 (0) 207 3689 334
e-mail: Richard.De.Silva@iqpc.co.uk

Kevin Duffey is Managing Director of the Cyber Rescue Alliance, a Membership organisation that helps CEOs lead recovery from cyber attack. Cyber Rescue operates in nine countries across Europe, helping leaders protect reputation and revenues when hackers break through. Members benefit from Executive Role Plays, bespoke Commercial Response Plans and expert coaching during a catastrophic breach. Cyber Research's advisors have led response to thousands of cyber attacks and hundreds of breaches. The Cyber Rescue team have expertise in the many functional areas that are impacted by a successful cyber attack; for example, Legal, PR, Hr, Operations, Finance and Customer Service, as well as IT Forensics and Remediation.

Cyber Rescue Alliance
4 Bonhill Street, London EC2A 4BX
Tel: +44 (0) 207 859 4320
e-mail: kevin.duffey@cyberrescue.co.uk

Jonathan Reuvid is the editorial director and a partner of Legend Business Books Ltd. A graduate of Oxford University (MA, PPE) he embarked on a second career in publishing in 1989 after a career in industry including Director of European Operations of the manufacturing division of a Fortune 500 multinational and joint venture development in China. Jonathan has more than 80 editions of more than 30 titles to his name as editor and part-author. He is a director of IPR Events London Ltd, the conference and exhibition management company and chairs the Community First Oxfordshire charity.

Legend Business Books Ltd
107-111 Fleet Street, London EC4A 2AB
Tel: +44 (0) 207 936 9941
e-mail: jreuvidembooks@aol.com

Richard Preece is a "hybrid" consultant and leader, who connects business and technical leadership so they can maximise the opportunities and minimize the risks of the Digital Age; in particular, by taking an integrated approach to make organisations more agile and resilient. Due to his work, he is a co-opted core member of the new British Standard (BS 31111) Cyber Risk and Resilience – Guidance for Top Management.

Oakas Ltd
Wessex House, Teign Road, Newton Abbot, Devon TQ12 4AA
Tel: +44 (0) 207 127 5312
e-mail: richard.preece@oakas.co.uk

Don Randall served with the City of London Police from 1969-1995, with specific emphasis on fraud and counter terrorism. Following 13 years at JPMorgan Chase as Managing Director, he joined the Bank of England in 2008 and was appointed the Bank's first Chief Information Security Officer in 2013. Don is chairman of the "Sister Banks", City of London Crime Prevention Association and "Project Griffin" and a member of the City of London Crime Disorder Reduction Panel. He is also a member of the London First Security Advisory Board, Executive Member of the London Resilience Board, Chairman of the London Resilience Business Sector Panel and Co-founder and Vice Chairman of the Cross Sector Safety & Security Communications initiative. Don is a Fellow of the Security Institute and a Chartered Security Professional (CSyP). He has also served as an external lay member of the City of London Police Committee. In 2007, Don was awarded an MBE for services to law enforcement for the harmonisation of the public/private sectors. He was presented with a Security Excellence Award for Outstanding Contribution to the Security Profession in 2013 and in 2015 was a recipient of the International Police and Public Safety 9/11 Commendation Medal.

Don Randall Associates
44 Fitzwalter Road, Colchester, Essex CO3 3SX
Tel: +44 (0) 7836 275 484
e-mail: donrandallassociates@gmail.com

Raymond Romero has over 30 years' experience in Information Technology (IT) management. His experience includes a focus on information security and privacy policy, compliance and information security operations. Mr. Romero works as an IT executive at the Board of Governors of the Federal Reserve System and started his IT career at Bank of America. He also contributes as a speaker at information security and risk management conferences. He has a Master's degree in Cyber Security from University of Maryland University College and a Bachelor of Science in Business Administration from California Polytechnic State University, San Luis Obispo.

Raymond Romero
Federal Reserve Board, Washington, DC 20551-0001
Tel: +1 (0) 202 369 9379
e-mail: Raymond.romero@frb.gov

Dr. Peter Mitic is Head of Operational Risk Methodology, Banco Santander. He is responsible for model building for AMA operational risk R and statistical research, and is searching into methods for quantification of Reputation Risk.

Patrik Heuri has been responsible for Information Security Risk in private banking institutions for more than 15 years. He has developed best in class preventive threat management of people security risks and has a holistic experience in risk that includes credit, market and operational risks.

Steve Snaith is a Director of RSM Risk Assurance Services LLP and has over 18 years' experience in cyber security and IT audit and leads RSM's technology risk assurance team. Steven is a regular speaker on cyber security and risk, and is a member the British Standards Cyber Risk and Resilience standards development committee.

References for Chapter 2.2

About the FFIEC. (n.d.). Retrieved from Federal Financial Institutions Examination Council: https://www.ffiec.gov/about.htm

Appendix B: Mapping Cybersecurity Assessment Tool to NIST Cybersecurity Framework. (2015, June). Retrieved from FFIEC Cybersecurity Assessment Tool: https://www.ffiec.gov/pdf/ cybersecurity/FFIEC_CAT_App_B_Map_to_NIST_CSF_ June_2015_PDF4.pdf

Cybersecurity Framework Feedback – What We Heard and Next Steps. (2016, June 9). Retrieved from NIST: http://www.nist.gov/cyberframework/upload/Workshop-Summary-2016.pdf

Developing a Framework To Improve Critical Infrastructure Cybersecurity. (2013, February` 26). Retrieved from Federal Register: https://www.federalregister.gov/articles/2013/02/26/2013-04413/ developing-a-framework-to-improve-critical-infrastructure-cybersecurity

Executive Order 13636 – Improving Critical Infrastructure Cyber-security. (2013, February 13). Retrieved from White House: www.whitehouse.gov/the-press-office/2013/02/12/executive-order-improving-critical-infrastructure-cybersecurity

FFIEC Assessment Tool – Overview for Chief Executive Officers and Boards of Directors. (2015, June). Retrieved from FFIEC: https://www.ffiec.gov/pdf/cybersecurity/FFIEC_CAT_CEO_ Board_Overview_June_2015_PDF1.pdf

FFIEC IT Examination Handbook – Management. (n.d.). Retrieved from FFIEC: http://ithandbook.ffiec.gov/media/210375/managementbooklet2015.pdf

Framework for Improving Critical Infrastructure Cybersecurity V1.0. (2014, February 12). Retrieved from NIST: http://www.nist.gov/cyberframework/upload/cybersecurity-framework-021214.pdf

Miller, R. (2015, August 31). *FFIEC and NIST: A Comparison of Two Prevalent New Compliance Frameworks.* Retrieved from West Monroe Partners: http://blog.westmonroepartners.com/ffiec-and-nist-a-comparison-of-two-prevalent-new-compliance-frameworks/

National Institute of Standards and Technology (NIST). (2014, February 12). Retrieved from NIST Cybersecurity Framework Version 1.0: http://www.nist.gov/cyberframework/upload/cybersecurity-framework-021214.pdf

MORE CYBER TITLES BY LEGEND BUSINESS BOOKS LTD

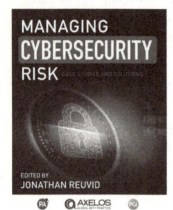

Paperback: 250 pages
ISBN: 978-1787198913
Format: 19 x 1.3 x 24.8 cm
Price: £39.99

This book will provide detailed information about the cyber security environment and specific threats. It will offer advice on the resources available to build defences and the selection of tools and managed services to achieve enhanced security at acceptable cost.

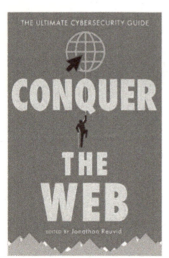

Paperback: 204 pages
ISBN: 978-1787198623
Format: 12.7 x 19.7 cm
Price: £14.99

This is the ultimate go to guide to understand and get practical advice on how to be safe and secure on the web.

This book covers areas such as,

• Building resilience into our IT Lifestyle
• Cyber Abuse: Scenarios & Stories
• Protecting Devices and downloading
• Gaming, gamble and travel
• Copycat websites
• Data protection and legislation
• Banking, apps and Passwords

BUSINESS PLANS THAT GET INVESTMENT
A Real-World Guide on How to Write a Business Plan

DAVID BATEMAN

Print: £14.99 | ISBN 978-1-785Ø793-2-Ø   Ebook: £5.99 | ISBN 978-1-785Ø793-3-7
Out Now

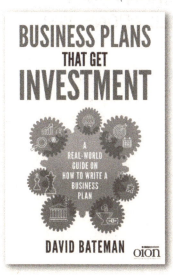

The Business Plan is an essential tool for attracting an investor's attention. They receive hundreds of plans every week and spend no more than ten minutes on each one before deciding if it is of further interest. This means that the plan needs to be a short, snappy document that conveys the facts about your business quickly and clearly.

This book explains how to write a plan that has the information that an investor needs to see. It shows that it is a simple process and anyone can do it, irrespective of background or prior knowledge.

Business Plans That Get Investment is a clear and comprehensive guide to writing a plan that turns those ten minutes of attention into investment.

"David's book is an invaluable resource for any entrepreneur seeking to raise funding. Based on years of experience, David shows how to keep things short and clear!"
—Thomas Hellmann, Professor of Entrepreneurship and Innovation, Saïd Business School, University of Oxford

"Anyone interested in this subject should read this book."
—Tim Hames, Director General of BVCA (British Venture Capital Association)

**FOR MORE INFORMATION ABOUT
LEGEND BUSINESS PUBLICATIONS, VISIT:**

WWW.LEGENDTIMESGROUP.COM/LEGEND-BUSINESS